The International Handbook of Electronic Commerce

The International Handbook of

Electronic Commerce

Revised Edition

Jae K Shim

GLOBAL
professional
publishing

Global Professional Publishing
Random Acres
Slip Mill Lane
Hawkhurst
Cranbrook
Kent TN18 5AD
Email: publishing@gppbooks.com

ISBN 978-1-906403-44-7

Printed by Good News Digital Books

Contents

What this Book will do for You

The International Handbook of Electronic Commerce is a valuable reference for business people, computer professionals, and consumers. Technology plays a vital role in business. Electronic commerce improves the efficiency and allow businesses to provide value and convenience to customers. The World Wide Web allows retailers to reach both their customers and suppliers and provides another medium for retailers to expand internationally at a relatively low cost.

This book covers all aspects of electronic commerce. It helps managers implement electronic commerce in their organization. It addresses the concerns of business managers such as security concerns. The book is designed as a practical, "how to" guide. We provide extensive examples to illustrate practical applications. The tools and techniques in this book can be adopted outright or modified to suit individual needs. Checklists, exhibits, illustrations, and step-by-step instructions enhance the book's practical use. Answers to commonly asked questions are given.

All types of businesses, not-for-profit entities and governmental bodies are using the World Wide Web. The Internet is an integral part of most transactions. Selling merchandise over the Internet reaches not only domestic consumers but also international consumers.

The future of retailing on the Internet greatly benefits consumers. Search engines enable consumers to find merchandise and services on the Internet with the lowest quoted price. Another technology assisting consumers in making purchases over the Internet is 3-D imaging. Instead of just reading a description and looking at a photograph, a consumer will be able to visually inspect the product at virtually any angle.

The combination of growth in the commercial utilization of the Internet, the rapid changes in technology, and the complexity of management has expanded the scope of the duties of business managers. To remain competitive, businesses must maintain a presence on the Internet. Business managers must keep up-to-date with changes in technology. This book provides business managers with an up-to-date compendium of current technologies and applications. New and emerging trends are considered.

Electronic commerce requires managers to be knowledgeable about both technology and its management. Special consideration has been given to balancing these two needs. We cover both traditional and emerging issues in technology and management of that technology.

This book is in an easy to understand and organized format. It is comprehensive and informative. It is a valuable reference that should be referred to on a daily basis.

About the Author

Dr. Jae K. Shim is a professor of business at California State University, Long Beach and CEO of Delta Consulting Company, a management consulting and training firm. Dr. Shim received his M.B.A. and Ph.D. degrees from the University of California at Berkeley (Haas School of Business). Dr. Shim has been a consultant to commercial and nonprofit organizations for over 30 years.

Dr. Shim has over 50 college and professional books to his credit, including, *The International Handbook of Computer Security, Data Management Systems, The Vest Pocket Guide of Information technology, Client/Server Computing for Business and Finance, The Artificial Intelligence Handbook,. The Vest-Pocket CPA, The Vest-Pocket CFO,* and the best-selling *Vest-Pocket MBA.*

Twenty six of his publications have been translated into foreign languages such as Chinese, Spanish, Russian, Polish, Croatian, Italian, Japanese, and Korean. Professor Shim's books have been published by Thompson-Southwestern, John Wiley, McGraw-Hill, Barron's, Commercial Clearing House (CCH), Prentice-Hall, American Management Association (Amacom), and the American Institute of CPAs (AICPA).

Dr. Shim has been frequently quoted by such media as the *Los Angeles Times, Orange County Register, Business Start-ups, Personal Finance, and Money Radio.* Dr. Shim has also published numerous articles in professional and academic journals. He was the recipient of the Financial Management Association International's *Credit Research Foundation Award* for his article on cash flow forecasting and financial modeling.

CHAPTER 1

The growth of electronic commerce (EC)

Electronic commerce (e-commerce, EC) is the buying and selling, marketing and servicing, and delivery and payment of products, services, and information over the Internet, intranets, extranets, and other networks, between an inter-networked enterprise and its prospects, customers, suppliers, and other business partners. The Internet and the World Wide Web allow millions of computers or other communication devices using different hardware, operating systems and software to link to each other by a common protocol. The information technology industry might see it as an electronic business application aimed at commercial transactions; in this context, it can involve electronic funds transfer, supply chain management, e-marketing, online marketing, online transaction processing, electronic data interchange (EDI), automated inventory management systems, and automated data collection systems.

On a global basis, it is estimated that 10 million host computers are connected into the Internet in over 160 countries. E-commerce transactions are done electronically and controlled from ordering to fulfillment. Electronic commerce is important in various interrelated areas such as business-to-business (B2B), customer-to-business (C2B), and intra-business. Business entities must rely on each other for such things as supplies, distribution, services, and technology. Networks link companies, customers, suppliers, employees, and distributors. Electronic Commerce (EC) growth can be attributed to global network of computers linked by high-speed to data lines and wireless systems.

According to the U.S. Census Bureau (www.census.gov), he estimate of U.S. retail e-commerce sales for the third quarter of 2008, adjusted for seasonal variation, but not for price changes, was $34.4 billion, an increase of 0.3 percent (±1.3%) from the second quarter of 2008. Total retail sales for the third quarter of 2008 were estimated at $1,018.8 billion, a decrease of 1.4 percent (±0.2%) from the second quarter of 2008. The third quarter 2008 e-commerce estimate increased 5.7 percent (±1.5%) from the third quarter of 2007 while total retail sales increased 0.3 percent (±0.5%) in the same period. E-commerce sales in the third quarter of 2008 accounted for 3.4 percent of total sales.

Total e-commerce sales for 2007 were estimated at $136.4 billion, an increase of 19.0 percent (±2.8%) from 2006. Total retail sales in 2007 increased 4.0 percent (±0.3%) from 2006. E-commerce sales in 2007 accounted for 3.4 percent of total sales. E-commerce sales in 2006 accounted for 2.9 percent of total sales.

The Roles of e-Business in Business

The Internet and related technologies and applications have changes the way businesses are operated and people work, and how information systems support business processes, decision making, and competitive advantage. Thus many businesses today are using Internet technologies to Web-enable business processes and create innovative e-business applications.

The Internet and Internet-like networks – inside the enterprise (intranets), and between an enterprise and its trading partners (extranets) – have become the primary information technology infrastructure that supports the e-business applications of many companies. These companies rely on e-business applications to:

▶ Reengineer internal business processes.
▶ Implement electronic commerce systems with their customers and suppliers.
▶ Promote enterprise collaboration among business teams and workgroups.

E-business is defined as the use of Internet technologies to internetwork and empower business processes, electronic commerce, and enterprise communication and collaboration within a company and with its customers, suppliers, and other business stakeholders. Enterprise collaboration systems involve the use of groupware tools to support communication, coordination, and collaboration among the members of networked teams and workgroups. An internetworked e-business enterprise depends on intranets, the Internet, extranets, and other networks to implement such systems.

Management must be abreast of recent developments in e-commerce. Electronic commerce changes and in some cases replaces nonelectronic ways of doing business, product and service delivery, and customer involvement. Organizational considerations include building infrastructure to share information, using intermediaries, and managing knowledge. EC involves many functional responsibilities including design, building, manufacturing, and controlling.

Business-people and information technology staff must be familiar with online applications in electronic commerce to effectively do their jobs and remain competitive. The ultimate survival and success of the business may depend on its involvement with EC. Staff must get involved with recent developments in interactivity and real time transactions. Staff must have a working knowledge of related hardware, software, and communications technology. They must know how transactions are processed and secured through electronic web-based systems. The business should be flexible when dealing with EC applications and usage. The objectives of EC include shorter manufacturing time, faster customer response, better service quality, cost reduction, and shorter product cycles.

Exhibit 1.1: Role of e-business in business

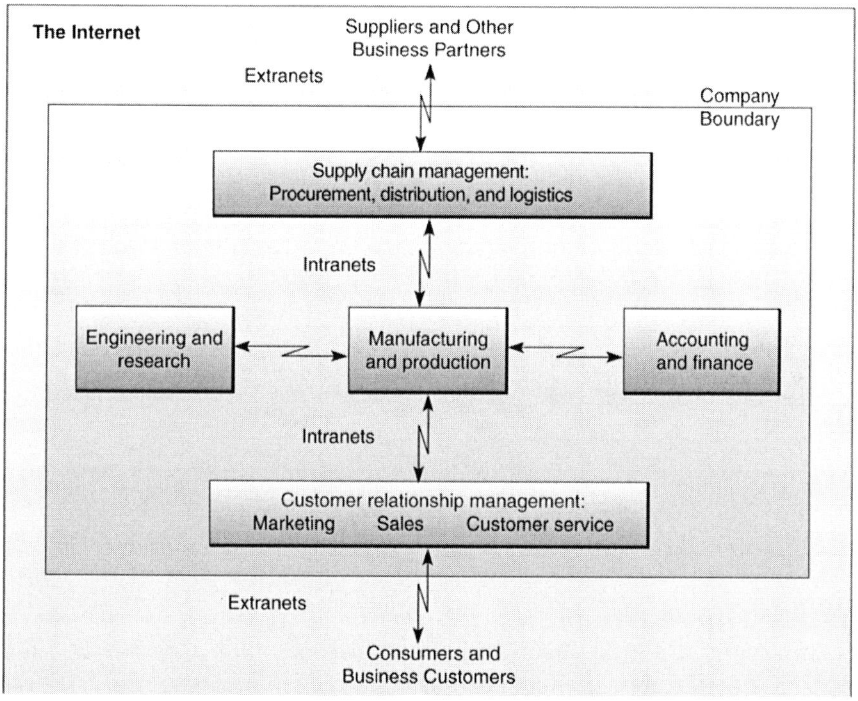

There are different definitions of EC depending on the perspective involved such as:
1. Business process viewpoint. The use of technology to automate business transactions and workflow.
2. Online viewpoint. The facilitation of the purchase and sale of goods or services over the Internet and other online services.

3. Communications viewpoint. The delivery of data, goods or services, computer network payments through telephone lines, and other communication modes.
4. Service perspective. The providing of quality services and products to satisfy the wants of business entities and customers consistent with the goals of reducing service costs and expediting delivery.

EC is of interest to business managers, marketers, accountants, financial executives, financial analysts, investors, creditors, lawyers, and consultants. The parties involved with EC include:

▶ Manufacturers, wholesalers, and retailers.
▶ Sellers of Internet commerce products such as Oracle, Microsoft, and Netscape.
▶ Financial institutions including banks.
▶ Insurance companies.
▶ Government regulatory agencies.
▶ Standards bodies.
▶ Industry associations.

Because of digitization, the electronic marketplace requires no physical stores or market institutions. The electronic marketplace allows for seller innovation of the entire business process from manufacturing to customer service. The ordering of goods and advertising are being digitized and carried out over the Internet. In other words, EC relates to sellers and buyers meeting to trade digital products with the use of digital processes. Products are being released from physical constraints and limitations into digital form to be delivered through the global network and paid for with digital currency. Whatever goods or services can be digitized or otherwise transferred electronically will find EC a very quick and cost effective means to reach consumers. Goods and services very suitable for EC include software (via electronic downloading to the consumer), video, cable television, music albums, books (via electronic transmission), newspapers and magazines (in electronic format), information databases, education and job training, home banking, bulletin boards and chat rooms.

E-commerce affects manufacturing, marketing, consumption, finance, and investments. There will be user interaction with products through downloading business problem solving software, exchange of personal settings, and e-mail. EC may be used for noncommercial functions such as filing and paying taxes, and personal finance.

Electronic commerce includes:

▶ Order processing to vendors. EC provides data about goods or services such as where to buy them, prices, warranty contracts, quantity available, delivery terms, and legal provisions. There is even online auctions for products such as eBay (electronic bay) which is a company having a giant virtual flea market. At the web site (www.ebay.com) companies and individuals trade their goods. For this service, eBay only gets a small transaction fee when a trade is made between the seller and buyer.

- Distribution of employee or product information such as through e-mail and the Web.
- Corporate financial management.
- Production logistics.
- Project performance and data.
- Online searches of information via search engines and/or surfing the Net.
- Personnel information.
- Warehousing information including inventory stocking levels.
- Online publishing of company information such as reports, analyses, and documents.
- Subscription services.
- Electronic mail and messaging. E-mail is the most widely used form of electronic commerce. About 75% of all online consumers use e-mail services.
- Inventory management and distribution.
- Order tracking.
- Examining shipments and deliveries.
- Obtaining information to prepare a competitive bid.
- There is electronic handling of the following:
- Production.
- Tracking and monitoring sales.
- Product and/or service selection and delivery. Being online allows for product selection and selling prices to be updated instantly.
- Advertising and promotion of online goods. For example, a new technology referred to as "virtual tags" allows consumers to view multimedia advertisements online and order a product just by clicking the mouse on the advertisement. Many goods and services lend themselves to being order via electronic catalogs such as computer products, food, travel services, and apparel.
- Application engineering.
- Payments. In an electronic payment system, a bill is sent electronically to a customer who then authorizes an electronic check. The customer's bank then electronically transfers funds from the customer's account to the biller's account. The customer receives electronic monthly statements listing the payments. With regard to electronic money.
- Consumer searches for product and service information.
- Marketing research.

▶ Shopping by online orders.
▶ Dissemination of product data.
▶ Accumulating customer data.
▶ Customer service and support.
▶ Pricing strategies.
▶ Financial services such as online investing in stocks.
▶ Distribution. For soft goods, distribution might simply be downloading while for hard goods distribution might be delivery.

Electronic data interchange (EDI) refers to the electronic purchase, receipt, and payment for inventory and supplies. EDI significantly reduces delivery time and related paper processing. Thus, reducing inventory and transaction costs.

Electronic data includes software. The following are suitable to Internet-based distribution: upgrades, program patches, and documentation.

Benefits of EC include:

▶ Eliminates limitations on place and time.
▶ Improves information flow.
▶ Fosters better customer relations and better product distribution.
▶ Allows data continuity which is having data created, altered, and distributed faster and at less cost. For example, companies can save money by using the Internet for business-to-business transactions than using private networks. Money can be saved from closing stores or less stocking of merchandise at existing stores by reducing overhead. Further, the company can minimize its transaction costs by improving the linkage between vendors, purchasers, and intermediaries. Areas of duplication may be eliminated along with better sharing of information to reduce costs.
▶ Stimulates sales and improves the revenue base in a number of ways including providing new markets, new information-oriented products and services, better channels of service delivery, and fostering interaction with customers.
▶ Reduces order processing time and inventory levels.
▶ Improves how business transactions are processed over networks. Such improvements result in better performance, better customer satisfaction, better management decisions, higher quality, enhanced efficiency, and better interaction.
▶ Provides business efficiencies such as upgrading technology, transferring content, transactional processing and payment, production processes, improved communication, more accurate transactions, better promotion and advertising, low-cost technological infrastructure, less obsolescence, enhanced sharing of information, and improved service.

▶ Better internal integration of the business entity's operations (e.g., improved interaction among departments within the company) as well as better external integration (linkage to the outside) taking the form of having a network of companies, contractors, suppliers and government agencies. With internal integration, there will be better coordination of decentralized decision making within the entity.

▶ Provides the opportunity for a business to move toward a virtual value chain and to two-way interactive communication.

In implementing EC, consideration should be given to the user's role, use of development mechanism, and nature of the applications. Implementation involves automating processes, using pilot projects, using data warehouses, and planning for growth and expansion.

Telecommunications companies such as wireless, satellite and land-based, cable-TV, and others are building the e-commerce communications infrastructure (information superhighway). Internet transmission speed (bandwidth), quality, and reliability must also be considered.

Internet service providers (ISPs) are the entities providing the basic connection to the Internet. There are numerous regional and local Internet service providers who provide custom web design, marketing, and other services besides e-commerce hosting services. ISPs offer "turnkey" e-commerce products in a single-ready-to-use package including hardware, software, payment processing and communications aspects. Turnkey solutions include providing for the connection, catalog maintenance, order and credit card processing, and other services. A determination must be made as to what information is on the company's computers and what reside with the ISP. How is information with the ISP controlled and secured?

A business may need to evaluate and decide whether to outsource some or all of their e-commerce functions. E-commerce offers opportunities for small businesses, too, by enabling them to market and sell at a low cost worldwide, thus allowing them to enter the global market right from start-up.

Mobile Commerce

Mobile commerce (m-commerce) is transactions conducted anywhere, anytime. M-commerce relies on the use of wireless communications to allow managers and corporations to place orders and conduct business using handheld computers, portable phones, laptop computers connected to a network, and other mobile devices. In addition to computers, many other devices can be connected to the Internet, including cell phones, PDAs, and home appliances. These devices also require specific protocols and approaches to connect. For example, *wireless application protocol (WAP)* is used to connect cell phones and other devices to the Internet.

CHAPTER 2

What is Electronic Commerce?

The term "electronic commerce" emerged only a few years ago when business people started to understand the powerful tool of the Internet. However, electronic commerce goes beyond simply "doing business electronically." Doing business electronically means that many conventional business processes, such as advertising and product ordering, are being digitized and conducted on the Internet. Beyond the basic idea of electronic commerce of "letting business people conduct business transactions over the Internet," new products have been released from their physical constraints and are being converted into digital products that can be delivered via the global network and paid for using digital currency. With digitization and digital payment systems, the electronic marketplace becomes a separate and independent market needing no physical presence for stores, products, sellers, or buyers. For example, a corporate buyer can browse the Internet, look at the merchandise on the Internet, and place an order. This transaction can be completed by sending a company's purchase order number to the vendor and receiving a confirmation number without a physical location.

Electronic Commerce of Digital Products

A market is composed of three components: players, products, and processes. Market players are sellers, buyers, intermediaries, and other third parties, such as governments and consumer advocacy groups. *Products* are the commodities to be exchanged. The interactions between market agents regarding products and other market activities are *processes,* which include product selection, production, market research, product search, ordering, paying, delivery, and consumption. These three components could be in the form of digital format (online) or in the form of physical format (offline). A traditional commerce has three components in physical format, while the core of electronic commerce has three components in digital format (see Exhibit 2.1). A business transaction may have both physical and digital components. For example, buying a book on the Internet has the following characteristics: The players and processes are digital, and the products are physical.

Exhibit 2.1: Comparison between e-commerce and traditional commerce

Market Components	Traditional Components	Electronic Components
Market players	Physical (a shopper in the department store)	Digital (an online shopper)
Products	Physical (a printed magazine)	Digital (an online magazine)
Processes	Physical (Buying books in a bookstore	

Market activities-from production, through distribution, to consumption--can occur online, bypassing all paper-based transactions and traditional communication media. This represents the future of electronic commerce. Although not all market components can be converted into digital format, most components can be more efficient if digital format is partially implemented. For example, a car with a smart device to display driving direction is both physical and digital.

The advantage of electronic commerce is that business transactions can be very efficient and fast. Entrepreneurs can use the Internet as the marketplace rather than huge retail channels (see Exhibit 2.2). However, other issues need to be researched, such as how to police the transactions over the network, how to certify the accuracy of each transaction, and how to prevent transaction fraud.

The Scope of e-Commerce

Companies involved in e-commerce as either buyers or sellers rely on Internet-based technologies and e-commerce applications and services to accomplish marketing, discovery, transaction processing, and product and customer service processes.

The Internet, intranets, and extranets provide vital electronic commerce links between the components of a business and its customers, suppliers, and other business partners. This allows companies to engage in three basic categories of electronic commerce applications:

Exhibit 2.2: The Internet

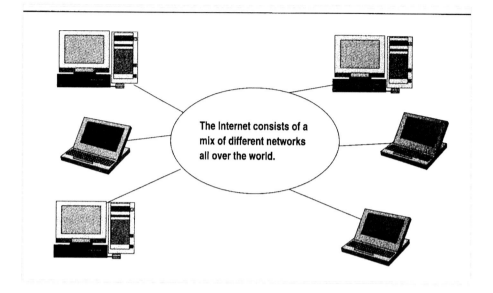

The Internet consists of a mix of different networks all over the world.

▶ **Business-to-Consumer (*B2C*) e-Commerce**:

In this form of electronic commerce, businesses must develop attractive electronic marketplaces to entice and sell products and services to customers. Companies may offer:

- ▶ e-commerce websites that provide virtual storefronts and multimedia catalogs
- ▶ Interactive order processing
- ▶ Secure electronic payment systems
- ▶ Online customer support

▶ *Business-to-Business (B2B) e-Commerce*:

This category of electronic commerce involves both electronic business marketplaces and direct market links between businesses. Companies may offer:

- ▶ Secure Internet or extranet e-commerce websites for their business customers and suppliers
- ▶ Electronic data interchange (EDI) via the Internet or extranets for computer-to-computer exchange of e-commerce documents with their larger business customers and suppliers
- ▶ B2B e-commerce portals that provide auction and exchange markets for businesses

▶ *Consumer-to-Consumer (C2C) e-Commerce*:

Successes of online auctions like e-Bay, allow consumers (and businesses) to buy and sell with each other in an auction process at an auction website.

▶ Online consumer or business auctions are an important e-commerce alternative for B2C or B2B e-commerce

▶ Electronic personal advertising of products or services to buy or sell by consumers at electronic newspaper sites, consumer e-commerce portals, or personal websites is an important form of C2C e-commerce

Business Applications in e-Commerce

From the inter-organizational perspective, electronic commerce facilitates the following business applications:

1. *Supplier management.* Electronic applications help companies reduce the number of suppliers and facilitate business partnerships by reducing purchase order (PO) processing costs and cycle times, and by increasing the number of POs processed with fewer people. In other words, this approach integrates a company's computer system with the vendor's by Internet technology.

2. *Inventory management.* Electronic applications shorten the order-ship-bill cycle.

3. *Distribution management.* Electronic applications facilitate the transmission of shipping documents such a bills of lading, purchase orders, advanced ship notices, and manifest claims, and enable better resource management by ensuring that the documents themselves contain more accurate data. Electronic commerce applications can also be used to process merchandise delivery services.

4. *Channel management.* Electronic applications quickly disseminate information about changing operational conditions to trading partners. By electronically linking production-related information with international distributor and reseller networks, companies can eliminate thousands of labor hours and ensure accurate information sharing.

5. *Payment management.* Electronic applications link companies with suppliers and distributors so the payments can be sent and received electronically. Electronic payment reduces clerical error, increases the speed at which companies compute invoices, and lower transaction fees and costs.

6. *Information management.* Information-oriented e-commerce allows change information on the net. Such applications allow users to retrieve and exchange information on the net and include chat room applications,

e-mail, news groups, net meetings, and other online information services. Organizations may post or publish corporate policies, product specifications, employee information, etc.

e-Commerce Technology, Infrastructure, and Development

For e-commerce to succeed, a complete set of hardware, software, and network components must be chosen carefully and integrated to support a large volume of transactions with customers, suppliers, and other business partners worldwide. Online consumers frequently complain that poor Web site performance (e.g., slow response time and "lost" orders) drives them to abandon some e-commerce sites in favor of those with better, more reliable performance. This section provides a brief overview of the key technology infrastructure components.

Hardware

A Web server complete with the appropriate software is key to successful c-commerce. The amount of storage capacity and computing power required of the Web server depends primarily on two things—the software that must run on the server and the volume of c-commerce transactions that must be processed. Although business managers and information systems staff can define the software to be used, it is difficult for them to estimate how much traffic the site will generate. As a result, the most successful c-commerce solutions arc designed to be highly scalable so that they can be upgraded to meet unexpected user traffic.

Many companies decide that a third-party Web service provider is the best way to meet their initial c-commerce needs. A Web service rents out space on its computer system and provides a high-speed connection to the Internet, which minimizes the initial setup costs for c-commerce. The service provider can also provide personnel trained to operate, troubleshoot, and manage the Web server. Other companies decide to take full responsibility for acquiring, operating, and supporting their own Web server hardware and software, but this approach requires considerable up-front capital and a set of skilled and trained individuals. Whichever approach is taken, there must be adequate hardware backup to avoid a major business disruption in case of a failure of the primary Web server.

Software

Each c-commerce Web server must have software to perform a number of fundamental services, including security and identification authentication, retrieval and sending of

Web pages, and Web page construction. The two most popular Web server software packages are Apache HTTP Server and Microsoft Internet Information Server.

Web site development tools include features such as an HTML/visual Web page editor (e.g., Microsoft's FrontPage, NetStudio's NetStudio, SofrQuad's HoTMetaL Pro), software development kits that include sample code and code development instructions for languages such as Java or Visual Basic, and Web page upload support to move Web pages from a development PC to the Web site. Which tools are bundled with the Web server software depends on which Web server software you select.

Web page construction software uses Web editors to produce Web pages—either static or dynamic. Static Web pages always contain the same information—for example, a page that provides text about the history of the company or a photo of corporate headquarters. Dynamic Web pages contain variable information and are built in response to a specific Web visitor's request. For example, if a Web site visitor inquires about the availability of a certain product by entering a product identification number, the Web server will search the product inventory database and generate a dynamic Web page based on the current product information it found, thus fulfilling the visitor's request. This same request by another visitor later in the day may yield different results due to ongoing changes in product inventory. A server that handles dynamic content must be able to access information from a variety of databases. The use of open database connectivity enables the Web server to assemble information from different database management systems, such as SQL Server, Oracle, and Informix.

Once you have located or built a host server, including the hardware, operating system, and Web server software, you can begin to investigate and install c-commerce software. There are three core tasks that c-commerce software must support: catalog management, product configuration, and shopping cart facilities.

Catalog management software combines different product data formats into a standard format for uniform viewing, aggregating, and integrating catalog data into a central repository for easy access, retrieval, and updating of pricing and availability changes. The data required to support large catalogs is almost always stored in a database on a computer that is separate from, but accessible to, the c-commerce server machine. The effort to build and maintain online catalogs can be substantial.

Corporate Express sells furniture, paper, computer supplies, and office equipment. It maintains catalogs tailored to each customer's format, terminology, and buying practices. If certain customers don't buy office furniture from Corporate Express, office furniture is blocked from their version of the catalog. Corporate Express also maintains a list of items that each customer orders frequently, as well as the special terms and prices that the customer has negotiated. Such attention to customization is greatly appreciated by customers because it makes their ordering process easier. Corporate buyers also appreciate the fact that their employees can only purchase prearranged items so that "maverick" buying is eliminated.

Customers need help when an item they are purchasing has many components and options. Product configuration software tools assist B2B salespeople with matching their company's products to customer needs. Buyers use the new Web-based product configuration software to build the product they need online with little or no help from salespeople. For example, Dell customers use product configuration software to build the computer of their dreams. Use of such software can expand into the service arena as well, with consumer loans and financial services to help people decide what sort of loan or insurance is best for them.

Today many c-commerce sites use an electronic shopping cart to track the items selected for purchase, allowing shoppers to view what is in their cart, add new items to it, or remove items from it. To order an item, the shopper simply clicks that item. All the details about it—including its price, product number, and other identifying information—are stored automatically. If the shopper later decides to remove one or more items from the cart, he or she can do so by viewing the cart's contents and removing any unwanted items. When the shopper is ready to pay for the items, he or she clicks a button (usually labeled "proceed to checkout") and begins a purchase transaction. Clicking the "Checkout" button displays another screen that usually asks the shopper to fill out billing, shipping, and payment method information and to confirm the order.

Internet Protocol Address

Just like telephone numbers, each computer that is connected to the Internet has a unique Internet protocol (IP) address. One IP address consists of 32 bits and is divided into four 8-bit segments, which are separated by a period. For example, "126.78.231.4" is an IP address that can uniquely identify a computer on the Internet. By typing in this address, users can access the site. If the Internet connection is temporarily set up, such as America Online users, the Internet server will temporarily assign an IP address for you.

Since the IP address is very hard to remember, a *domain name* corresponding to each address is used to reduce the complexity. A domain name consists of two levels: *top-level domain names* are classifications of different purposes of the usage. For example, "edu" stands for educational institute and "gov" stands for governments. Other top-level domain names include countries such as "us" (USA), "cn" (CHINA), and "mx" (MEXICO). The *lower-level domain name* is a unique name, which identifies the server. For example, IBM and FORD are lower-level domain names. The combination of the top-level domain name and the lower-level domain name can therefore identify the type of business and its country. For example, *wwwibm.com* represents that IBM is a commercial entity (.com), or *www.csulb.edu* states that "edu" is an educational institute. Unlike the IP address, there is no limit to the number of possible domain names. A single server may have several domain names as long as there is a way to map between domain names and their corresponding IP addresses. Such a database is kept in the DNS server, or name server, accessible by a router. In other words, after a user types in the domain name, it is transferred to a corresponding IP address and the server with that IP address is accessed.

The coordinator of domain names is known as the Internet Network Information Center, or InterNIC. This organization regulates the way domain names are used (see Exhibit 2.3).

Exhibit 2.3: The Components of a Domain Name

INTERNET COMPUTER SUFFIX*	ORGANIZATION TYPE	DOMAIN NAME	ENTITY
.com	Commercial organization	www.ibm.com	IBM Corporation
.edu	Academic institution	www.csulb.edu	California State University of Long Beach
.gov	Government agency	www.irs.gov	Internal Revenue Services
.mil	Military	www.army.mil	U.S. Army
.org	Nonprofit organization	www.acm.org	Association for Computing Machinery
.net	Internet service provider	www.earthlink.net	Earthlink

* we now have others: .info, .biz, .net, .pro, .name, and .tv.

EXAMPLES FROM OTHER COUNTRIES	
.cn	China
.au	Australia
.jp	Japan
.uk	United Kingdom

Internet Service Provider and Other Services

The original goal of the Internet was to connect military computers with redundant communication routes during a war. This network ensures that communications can be carried on even if part of the network is not functional. Since 1991, the National Science Foundation eased the restriction of accessing the Internet, and commercial access became available. Since then, the traffic and activities on the Internet have grown exponentially. Companies and individuals can access the Internet through many service providers. The service providers can provide simple access, value-added service, or presence on the Internet.

Internet Service Providers

An Internet service provider (ISP) is any company that provides individuals and organizations with access to the Internet. ISPs do not offer the extended informational services offered by commercial online services such as America Online or Earthlink. There are literally thousands of Internet service providers, ranging from universities making unused communications line capacity available to students and faculty to major communications giants such as AT&T and MCI. To use this type of connection, you must have an account with the service provider and software that allows a direct link via TCP/IP.

To use an ISP such as MSN, you must have an account with the service provider and software that allows a direct link via TCP/IP. In choosing an Internet service provider, users consider these important criteria: cost, reliability, security, availability of enhanced features, and the service provider's general reputation. Reliability is critical because if your connection to the ISP fails, it interrupts your communication with customers and suppliers. Among the value-added services ISPs provide are electronic commerce, networks to connect employees, networks to connect with business partners, host computers to establish your own Web site, Web transaction processing, network security and administration, and integration services. Many corporate IS managers welcome the chance to turn to ISPs for this wide range of services because they do not have the in-house expertise and cannot afford the time to develop such services from scratch. In addition, when organizations go with an ISP-hosted network, they can also tap the ISP's national infrastructure at minimum cost. That is important when a company has offices spread across the country.

In most cases, ISPs charge a monthly fee that can range from $15 to $30 for unlimited Internet connection through a standard modem. The fee normally includes e-mail. Some ISPs, however, are experimenting with low-fee or no-fee Internet access. But there are strings attached to the no-fee offers in most cases. Some free ISPs require

17

that customers provide detailed demographic and personal information. In other cases, customers must put up with extra advertising. For example, a pop-up ad is a window that is displayed when someone visits a Web site. It pops up and advertises a product or service. Some c-commerce retailers have posted ads that resemble computer-warning messages and have been sued for deceptive advertising. A banner ad appears as a banner or advertising window that you can ignore or click to go to the advertiser's Web site.

Internet Presence Providers

Internet presence providers provide Internet presence by hosting the user's web pages on the Internet. Some companies provide an Internet mall with spaces for various vendors to sell their products. Vendors pay a fee plus the traffic charge and receive a space for an electronic store, which is actually disk space where the store's web site is saved. Therefore, online transactions can be made on the network.

Essential e-Commerce Processes

The nine essential e-commerce processes required for the successful operation or management of e-commerce activities consist of:

- Access control and security
- Profiling and personalizing
- Search management
- Content management
- Catalog management
- Payment
- Workflow management
- Event notification
- Collaboration and trading

Access Control and Security

E-commerce processes must establish mutual trust and secure access between the parties in an e-commerce transaction by authenticating users, authorizing access, and enforcing security features.

Profiling and Personalization

Profiling processes gather data on an individual and their website behaviour and choices, and build electronic profiles of their characteristics and preferences. User profiles are developed using profiling tools such as user registration, cookie files, website behaviour tracking software, and user feedback.

Search Management

Efficient and effective search processes provide a top e-commerce website capability that helps customers find the specific product or service they want to evaluate or buy.

Content and Catalog Management

Content management software helps e-commerce companies develop, generate, deliver, update, and archive text data, and multimedia information at e-commerce websites. E-commerce content frequently takes the form of multimedia catalogs of product information. Generating and managing catalog content is a major subset of content management.

Content and catalog management may be expanded to include product configuration processes that support Web-based customer self—service and the mass customization of a company's products. Configuration software helps online customers select the optimum feasible set of product features that can be included in a finished product.

Workflow Management

E-business workflow systems help employees electronically collaborate to accomplish structured work tasks within knowledge-based business processes. Workflow management in both e-business and e-commerce depends on a workflow software engine containing software models of the business processes to be accomplished. The workflow model expresses the predefined sets of business rules, roles of stakeholders, authorization requirements, routing alternatives, databases used, and sequence of tasks required for each e-commerce process.

Event Notification

Most e-commerce applications are event-driven systems that respond to a multitude of events. Event notification processes play an important role in e-commerce systems, since customers, suppliers, employees, and other stakeholders must be notified of all events that might affect their status in a transaction.

Collaboration and Trading

This category of e-commerce processes are those that support the vital collaboration arrangements and trading services needed by customers, suppliers, and other stakeholders to accomplish e-commerce transactions.

Electronic Payments Processes

Payments for the products and services purchased are an obvious and vital step in the electronic commerce transaction process. Concerns of electronic payments and security include:

- The near-anonymous electronic nature of transactions taking place between the networked computer systems of buyers and sellers, and the security issues involved.
- Electronic payment process is complex because of the wide variety of debit and credit alternatives and financial institutions and intermediaries that may be part of the process.
- Varieties of **electronic payment systems** have evolved. New payment systems are being developed and tested to meet the security and technical challenges of electronic commerce over the Internet.

Web Payment Processes

Most e-commerce systems on the Web involving businesses and consumers (B2C) depend on credit card payment processes. Buy many B2B e-commerce systems rely on more complex payment processes based on the use of purchase orders. Both types of e-commerce typically use an electronic *shopping cart* process, which enables customers to select products from website catalog displays and put them temporarily in a virtual shopping basket for later checkout and processing.

Electronic Funds Transfer

Electronic funds transfer (EFT) systems are a major form of electronic commerce systems in banking and retailing industries. EFT systems use a variety of information technologies to capture and process money and credit transfers between banks and businesses and their customers. EFT transaction costs are lower than for manual systems because documents and human intervention are eliminated from the transactions process.

Secure Electronic Payments

When you make an online purchase on the Internet, your credit card information is vulnerable to interception by *network sniffers*, software that easily recognizes credit card number formats. Several basic security measures are being used to solve this security problem. They include:

- Encrypt (code and scramble) the data passing between the customer and merchant
- Encrypt the data passing between the customer and the company authorizing the credit card transaction

▷ Take sensitive information offline

Security methods developed include:

▷ **Secure Socket Layer** (SSL) - automatically encrypts data passing between your Web browser and a merchant's server.

▷ **Digital Wallet** - you add security software add-on modules to your Web browser. This enables your browser to encrypt your credit card data in such a way that only the bank that authorizes credit card transactions for the merchant can see it.

▷ **Secure Electronic Transaction (SET)** - software encrypts a *digital envelope* of *digital certificates* specifying the payment details for each transaction. SET is expected to become the dominant standard for secure electronic payments on the Internet.

The Internet and the Intranet

The Internet

What Is the Internet? In 1969, the U.S. Department of Defense's Advanced Research Projects Agency (ARPA) wanted to establish a communications network that would operate in case of a nuclear strike, as an alternative to telephone, radio, and television, all of which might quickly become nonfunctional in a military crisis. The most important feature of ARPANET is that it has no central point for controlling communications. One message can be transmitted to another location through any possible routes so that in case one route is destroyed, the message can still be transmitted. ARPANET's computers exchange information in the form of digitized data, operating according to standards agreed upon by all participants, with no one person, institution, or organization in charge. Since the ARPANET uses open system design, this network had a dramatic growth in the last several years and that became the Internet.

Today, the Internet is a network of networks with hundreds of thousands of servers. Tens of millions of people take for granted that, with a simple phone call via their modems, they can access a huge number of files of all types from all Internet servers, do research, purchase merchandise, and participate in discussion forums with someone in another country.

Internet2

Internet2 is a high-performance network that uses an entirely different infrastructure than the public Internet we know today. There are over 200 universities and scientific institutions and over 60 communications corporations in the Internet2 network.

Internet2 is never intended to replace the internet, rather its purpose is to build a road map that can be followed when the next stage of innovation to the current Internet takes place.

Most institutions and commercial partners are connected via Abilene, a network backbone that will soon support throughput of 10 gigabits per second. In short, Internet2 is all about high-speed telecommunications and infinite bandwidth.

Intranet

Intranet is defined as an enterprise-owned network that uses an Internet interface for information exchange and sharing. In other words, Intranet is a private, small-scale version of the Internet. It is mainly designed to perform functionality within the enterprise by using a common infrastructure of the Internet. (see Exhibit 2.4).

An intranet is protected by security measures such as passwords, encryption designed to perform functionality within the enterprise by using a common infrastructure of the same tools, and fire walls, and thus can only be accessed by authorized users through the Internet. A company's intranet can also be accessed through the intranets of customers, suppliers, and other business partners via extranet links. Since intranets are Internet-like networks within organizations, they depend on all of the information technologies that make the Internet possible.

These include:
► TCP/IP client/server networks
► Hardware and software such as Web browsers and server suites
► HTML Web publishing software
► Network management and security programs
► Hypermedia databases

Exhibit 2.4: How the Internet is connected to an Intranet

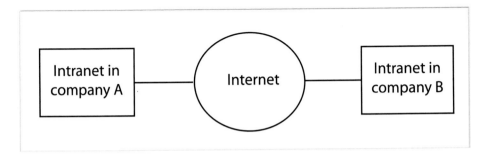

Exhibit 2.5 presents practical applications of Intranets and Extranets.

Exhibit 2.5: Practical Applications of Intranets/Extranets

▷ Providing managers with accounting, audit, and tax information	▷ Providing project, proposal, and scheduling data to participating companies in joint ventures
▷ Providing marketing and sales information to current and prospective customers	▷ Providing press releases and product/service announcements
▷ Furnishing information to salespersons in the field and managers at different branches	▷ Giving legal information to outsider attorneys involved in litigation matters
▷ Furnishing resource needs and reports to supplies	▷ Providing trade associations with input for their surveys
▷ Communicating corporate information to employees such as company policies and forms, operating instructions, job documents, business plans, and newsletters	▷ Furnishing information to outside consultants (e.g. investment management advisors, pension planners)
▷ Assisting in employee training and development	▷ Providing insurance companies with information to draft or modify insurance coverage
▷ Transferring information to government agencies (e.g., Department of Commerce, SEC, IRS)	▷ Furnishing economic statistics about the company to economic advisors
▷ Furnishing current and prospective investors with profitability, growth, and market value statistics	▷ Providing spreadsheets, database reports, tables, checklists, and graphs to interested parties
▷ Providing lenders and creditors with useful liquidity and solvency ratios	▷ Displaying e-mail

Internet and Telecommunications Services

A wide variety of services are available to help individuals and organizations tap the power of the Internet.

E-Mail and Instant Messaging

E-mail has changed the way people communicate. It improves the efficiency of communications by reducing interruptions from the telephone and unscheduled personal contacts. Also, messages can be distributed to multiple recipients easily and quickly without the inconvenience and delay of scheduling meetings. Because past messages can be saved, they can be reviewed later. And because messages are received at a time convenient to the recipient, the recipient has time to respond more clearly and to the point. Many people have two or more e-mail addresses, including free e-mail services.

For large organizations whose operations span a country or the world, e-mail allows people to work around time zone changes. Some users of e-mail estimate that they eliminate two hours of verbal communications for every hour of e-mail use.

The federal government and some states are now proposing legislation to block unwanted e-mail. California, for example, has proposed legislation that would prevent companies from sending unsolicited, commercial e-mail to California residents. The U.S. Congress passed a federal law, called Controlling the Assault of Non Solicited Pornography and Marketing Act (CAN SPAM), to reduce spam sent by companies in the United States. Unfortunately, legitimate e-mail can get lost. An informal survey of about 10,000 individuals revealed that up to 40 percent of legitimate e-mails are not getting to their proper destinations.

Instant messaging is online, real-time communication between two or more people who are connected to the Internet. With instant messaging, two or more screens open up. Each screen displays what one person is typing. Because the typing is displayed on the screen in real time, it is like talking to someone using the keyboard.

A number of companies offer instant messaging, including America Online, Yahoo!, and Microsoft. America Online is one of the leaders in instant messaging, with about 40 million users of its Instant Messenger and about 50 million people using its client program ICQ In addition to being able to type messages on a keyboard and have the information instantly displayed on the other person's screen, some instant messaging programs are allowing voice communication or connection to cell phones. A wireless service provider announced that **it** has developed a technology that can detect when a person's cell phone is turned on. With this technology, someone on the Internet can use instant messaging to communicate with someone on a cell phone anywhere in the world. Apple is experimenting with adding audio and video to its instant messaging service, called iChat. The iSight camera can be used to transfer visual images through instant messaging.

Instant messaging services often use a *buddy list* that alerts people when their friends are also online. This feature makes instant messaging even more useful. Instant messaging is so popular that **it** helps Internet service providers and online services draw new customers and keep old ones.

Internet Mobile Phones and Handheld Computers

Increasingly, mobile phones, handheld computers, and other devices are being connected to the Internet. Some mobile phones, for example, can be connected to the Internet to allow people to search for information, buy products, and chat with business associates and friends. A sales manager for a computer company can use her cell phone to check her company's Internet site to see whether there are enough desktop computers in inventory to fill a large order for an important customer. Using Short Message Service, people can send brief text messages of up to 160 characters between two or more mobile phone users.

The service is often called *texting*. Some cell phones also come equipped with digital cameras, FM radios, video games, and small color screens to watch TV. Using multimedia messaging service (MMS), people can send pictures, video, and audio over cell phones to other cell phones or Internet sites. An insurance investigator can use MMS to send photos of a car accident to a central office to process an insurance claim. Of course, cell phones can also be used to send e-mail messages to others. Legislation passed in fall 2003 allows cell phone users to keep their phone numbers when switching to another cell phone company.

In addition to cell phones, handheld computers and other devices can also be connected to the Internet using phone lines or wireless connections, such as Wi-Fi. After connecting, these devices have full access to the Internet and all its applications, which are discussed in this chapter and throughout the book. Managers use handheld computers, such as the BlackBerry or Treo handheld computer, and the Internet to check business e-mail when they are out of the office; sales representatives use them to demonstrate products to customers, check product availability and pricing, and upload customer orders.

Web Log (Blog)

A Web log, also called a blog, is a Web site that people can create and use to write about their observations, experiences, and feelings on a wide range of topics. A *blogger* is a person who creates a blog, while *blogging* refers to the process of placing entries on a blog site. A blog is like a journal. When people post information to a blog, it is placed at the top of the blog. Previous entries on the blog are pushed down. Blogs can be used by anyone or any organization to publish and share information.

Blogs exist in a wide variety of topics and areas. For example, the Western States Information Network (WSIN) developed a blog to allow local fire departments, water departments, and similar organizations to share information online. E-mails between departments are posted on the blog. The blog provides a central location where all e-mails can be posted and read. Blogs are used by journalists, people in disaster areas, soldiers in the field, and people who just want to express themselves. Venture capitalists can use *www.ventureblog.com* to investigate Internet or dot.com companies. Blog sites, such as *www.blogger.com* and *www.globeqfblogs.com* can include information and tools to help people create and use Web logs. Blogs are easy to set up. You can go to a blog service provider, such as *www.livejournal.com,* create a username and password, select a theme, choose a URL, follow any other instructions, and start making your first entry. Below is a list of blog sites related to money and personal finance matters:

- ▶ **www.seekingalpha.com.** The mother of all investment blogs with links to everything stock market, venture capital, and economics.
- ▶ **www.pfblog.com.** It's full of personal-finance and investing tips, well organized, with links to many, many other money blogs.
- ▶ **www.soundmoneytips.com.** This has a list of most financial blogs and it's also a money tips blog of its own. Plus, it appears to have a writer and an editor. Consequently, it's shorter, snappier, and smarter than a lot of the competition.
- ▶ **www.fivecentnickel.com.** Short and sweet and focused on family finances.
- ▶ **www.allthingsfinancial.blogspot.com.** A fee-only financial planner's musings on stocks, savings, inspirational books and more.
- ▶ **www.frugalforlife.blogspot.com.** Where the self-proclaimed cheapskates chill. Lots of links and content for folks who are convinced they can save as much through smart household management as they can make in the stock market.

Chat Rooms

A chat room is a facility that enables *two* or more people to engage in interactive "conversations" over the Internet. When you participate in a chat room, dozens of people from around the world might be participating. Multiperson chats are usually organized around specific topics, and participants often adopt nicknames to maintain anonymity. One form of chat room, Internet Relay Chat (IRC), requires participants to type their conversation rather than speak. Voice chat is also an option, but you must have a microphone, sound card and speakers, fast modem or broadband, and voice-chat software compatible with the other participants'.

Internet Phone and Videoconferencing Services

Internet phone service enables you to communicate with others around the world. This service is relatively inexpensive and can make sense for international calls. With some services, it is possible to make a call from someone using the Internet to someone using a standard phone. Cost is often a big factor in use of Internet phones—a call can be as low as 1 cent per minute for calls within the United States. Low rates are also available for calling outside the United States. In addition, voice mail and fax capabilities are available. Some cable TV companies, for example, are offering cable TV, phone service, and caller ID for under $40 a month.

Using *voice-over-IP (VoIP)* technology, network managers can route phone calls and fax transmissions over the same network they use for data—which means no more separate phone bills. Gateways installed at both ends of the communications link convert voice to IP packets and back. With the advent of widespread, low-cost Internet telephony services, traditional long-distance providers are being pushed to either respond in kind or trim their own long-distance rates. The school system in Appleton, Wisconsin, for example, installed a phone system based on the Internet and saved about 30 percent a year in telecommunications costs.

What is especially interesting about VoIP is the way voice is being merged with video and data communications over the Web or a company's data network In the long run, it's not the cost savings that will boost the market, it's the multimedia capabilities **it** gives us and the smart call-management capabilities. Travel agents could use voice and video over the Internet to discuss travel plans; Web merchants could use **it** to show merchandise and take orders; and customers could show suppliers problems with their products.

Internet videoconferencing, which supports both voice and visual communications, is another important Internet application. Microsoft NetMeeting, a utility within Windows, is an inexpensive and easy way for people to meet and communicate on the Web. The Internet can also be used to broadcast sales seminars using presentation software and videoconferencing equipment. These Internet presentations are often called *Webcasts* or *Webinars*. Hardware and software are needed to support videoconferencing. The key here is a video codec to convert visual images into a stream of digital bits and translate back again. The ideal video product will support multipoint conferencing, in which multiple users appear simultaneously on multiple screens.

Content Streaming

Content streaming is a method for transferring multimedia files over the Internet so that the data stream of voice and pictures plays more or less continuously, without a break, or with very few of them. It also enables users to browse large files in real time.

For example, rather than wait the half-hour **it** might take for an entire 5-MB video clip to download before they can play **it,** users can begin viewing a streamed video as it is being received.

GSS Software

GSS software, often called *groupware* or *workgroup software,* helps with joint workgroup scheduling, communication, and management. One popular package, Lotus Notes, can capture, store, manipulate, and distribute memos and communications that are developed during group projects. Some companies standardize on messaging and collaboration software, such as Lotus Notes. Microsoft's NetMeeting product supports application sharing in multiparty calls. Microsoft Exchange is another example of groupware. This software allows users to set up electronic bulletin boards, schedule group meetings, and use e-mail in a group setting.

NetDocuments Enterprise can be used for Web collaboration. The groupware is intended for legal, accounting, and real estate businesses. A Breakout Session feature allows two people to take a copy of a document to a shared folder for joint revision and work. The software also permits digital signatures and the ability to download and work on shared documents on handheld computers. Other GSS software packages include Collabra Share, OpenMind, and TeamWare. All of these tools can aid in group decision making.

In addition to stand-alone products, GSS software is increasingly being incorporated into existing software packages. Today, some transaction processing and enterprise resource plan-fling packages include collaboration software. Some ERP producers, for example, have developed groupware to facilitate collaboration and to allow users to integrate applications from other vendors into the ERP system of programs. Today, groupware can interact with wireless devices. Research In Motion, the maker of Blackberry software, offers mobile communications, access to group information, meeting schedules, and other services that can be directly tied to groupware and servers. In addition to groupware, GSSs use a number of tools discussed previously, including the following:

- E-mail and instant messaging
- Videoconferencing
- Group scheduling
- Project management
- Document sharing

GSS Alternatives

Group support systems can take on a number of network configurations, depending on the needs of the group, the decision to be supported, and the geographic location of group members. The frequency of GSS use and the location of the decision makers are two important factors.

The Decision Room

The decision room is ideal for situations in which decision makers are located in the same building or geographic area and the decision makers are occasional users of the GSS approach. In these cases, one or more decision rooms or facilities can be set up to accommodate the GSS approach. Groups, such as marketing research teams, production management groups, financial control teams, or quality-control committees, can use the decision rooms when needed. The decision room alternative combines face-to-face verbal interaction with technology-aided formalization to make the meeting more effective and efficient. Decision rooms, however, can be expensive to set up and operate.

The Local Area Decision Network

The local area decision network can be used when group members are located in the same building or geographic area and under conditions in which group decision making is frequent. In these cases, the technology and equipment of the GSS approach is placed directly into the offices of the group members. Usually this is accomplished via a local area network (LAN).

The Teleconferencing Alternative

Teleconferencing is used when the decision frequency is low and the location of group members is distant. These distant and occasional group meetings can tie together multiple GSS decision-making rooms across the country or around the world. Using long-distance communications technology, these decision rooms are electronically connected in teleconferences and videoconferences. This alternative can offer a high degree of flexibility. The GSS decision rooms can be used locally in a group setting or globally when decision makers are located throughout the world. GSS decision rooms are often connected through the Internet.

The Wide Area Decision Network

The wide area decision network is used when the decision frequency is high and the location of group members is distant. In this case, the decision makers require frequent or constant use of the GSS approach. Decision makers located throughout the country or the world must be linked electronically through a wide area network (WAN). The group facilitator and all group members are geographically dispersed. In some cases, the model base and database are also geographically dispersed. This GSS alternative allows people to work in virtual workgroups, in which teams of people located around the world can work on common problems.

Web Servers

A web server is a computer that hosts all web sites so that other users can access the information through the Internet. Information in the web paradigm is provided or published on a web server. Web servers are principally used to maintain a directory of web pages. A web server could use the Unix system as its operating system, called a Unix server, or the Microsoft Windows NT operating system as an NT server.

The major responsibility of a server is to respond to requests from clients' or users' computers via a browser. Essentially, web servers release information to the users when the users send requests through the browser. If the web server breaks down, web pages and all applications will not be available to users.

Web Browsers and Search Engines

A web browser is the vehicle that allows users to browse the World Wide Web. Users simply type in the address of a specific web server's web page (the URL) in the designated retrieve area, and the web browser locates the web server to request the web page addressed. The web browser then waits, usually only seconds, until the request information is sent back from the web server. The user can then view the information through the web server.

Among many browsers available in the market, the most popular is Microsoft Internet Explorer. Others include Mozilla, Firefox, Safari, Netscape, and Opera in order of descending popularity. All of them offer a suite of functions that assists the user's everyday needs, including a bookmark catalog for organizing the addresses of frequently visited web sites, e-mail, a newsreader, and setup scripts for Internet service providers. Web browsers allow one to access corporate information over the existing network. Employees in different divisions of the company located in different geographic areas can access and use centralized or scattered information. Along with the growth of the web, browser usage has risen dramatically.

A variety of search sites are available on the Internet to make accessing Internet resources if not painless, at least more pleasant and productive. Basically, these sites fall into two categories—directories for browsing the Internet and indexes for searching for specific information.

Browsing the Internet Web directories are hyperlinked lists of websites, hierarchically organized into topical categories and subcategories. Clicking your way through these lists will lead you to website links for the subject you're investigating. Use these directories when you need to find common information that can be easily classified. If you aren't looking for something very specific, try moving down through the general categories listed to reach a more specific category (in computer language, to "drill down"). In this way, you can narrow your search.

Searching the Internet Web indexes are massive, computer-generated databases containing information on millions of webpages and usenet newsgroup articles. By entering keywords or phrases, you can retrieve lists of webpages that contain your search term. The lists are created by Web crawlers (also called robots or spiders), software programs that roam the Web, looking for new sites by following links from page to page. Once your query executes, the Web search site displays the list of hits as a page containing the URLs (Universal Resource Locators, or Internet addresses) that are hyperlinked. Popular search engines include Google, Yahoo, and MSN.

The success of your Internet search will depend on how skillfully you choose your keywords (or search terms). Remember that the computer makes a very literal search; it will find exactly what you ask for—and nothing more. If you use the search term secretaries, many search indexes will not find citations for the words secretary or secretarial. Some indexes have a feature known as truncation, which allows you to search for the root of a term. Thus, a search for secre would retrieve secret, secretarial, secretaries, secretary, secretion, and so on. You would then choose the entries appropriate for your purpose.

One of the most common mistakes people make is to use too few keywords in their searches or to use the wrong kinds of keywords. (Too many hits is just as unhelpful as too few hits.) Generally, try to identify three or four keywords—and use nouns. The only time you generally need to use adjectives or adverbs is if the term itself contains one—such as World Wide Web (and don't forget to put phrases in quotation marks).

CHAPTER 3

World Wide Web and Electronic Commerce

It seems almost ironic that technology spawned from the military and political minds wrapped up in the Cold War has become arguably the single greatest advance in the business world in the 20th Century. Originally designed as a channel through which the United States government could share post-apocalyptic information, the Internet, and its spin-off network the World Wide Web, have become an integral part of day-to-day business around the world. Since the National Science Foundation lifted its ban on commercial use of the Internet in 1991, this advanced computer network has rapidly become much more important to today's business world than it ever was as part of the government infrastructure.

With the transformation of the Internet and the World Wide Web into much more user friendly business models the resulting explosion in their popularity spurred the development of a radically new method of conducting business transactions. The revolution of electronic commerce (E-commerce) has since completely reshaped the business world's approach to consumer interaction and business transaction.

The Rise of the Internet and the World Wide Web

The theory behind the Internet has its roots in the Cold War of the early 1960's, and the perceived need for a decentralized computer network that would enable the

United States government to maintain open lines of communication in a post-nuclear apocalyptic society.

Researchers felt that a decentralized computer network consisting of multiple-location computer nodes connected to each other via a backbone of high-traffic telephone lines would present too many targets for the Soviet Union to take out in the event of a Nuclear War. This network, dubbed the ARPANET, would survive through its collection of nodes even in the event that several of the nodes were destroyed. From this initial concept, it is not difficult to foresee the numerous ways in which a computer network connecting businesses and consumers in much the same way would be invaluable to business communication and sales.

By the end of the decade advances in the ARPANET would spawn what has become the Internet. The new system was designed as crude newswire to handle the transfer of news articles between nodes. The year 1972 proved to be a monumental year in the development of the ARPANET and specifically the spawning of the Internet. In that one year, the first computer-to-computer chat took place, the first electronic mail program was developed, and the first public demonstration of ARPANET using Internet protocols took place in San Francisco. The following year the system went international as additional nodes were set up in Europe.

Over the next decade advances in Internet technology enabled business to begin to take advantage of this new network. The development of an Electronic Data Interchange (EDI) allowed businesses to communicate via proprietary networks between manufacturers, suppliers, and sellers. The EDI presented the first case of business using the Internet to open up better lines of interoffice communication. Business was now on-line and in time over 100,000 companies developed some level EDI. While EDI empowered business partners to share information on sales, inventory, shipping, and other project information, developing these proprietary networks proved to be tremendously expensive and therefore only available and cost-effective to the largest of companies. However, this was all about to change in 1984.

In 1984 the National Science Foundation, which was the administrator of the nation's network backbone, developed a new network separate from the Internet. The new NSFNET backbone marked the beginning of what would become the World Wide Web. By the end of the decade the first relays between a commercial electronic mail carrier and the Internet had taken place. The year 1990 proved to be another landmark year in the development of the Internet and the World Wide Web as 'The World' became the first commercial provider of dial-up access, and later the same year the first remotely operated machine was hooked to the Internet. The 'Internet Toaster' was to be the ancestor of the present server based system that the World Wide Web is now based. Despite these tremendous developments in the World Wide Web and Internet technology, the NSF still maintained complete control of the two fledgling networks. Up until 1991, the NSF had implemented a commercial ban on Internet use. The lifting of the commercial ban on the Internet was like opening the flood gates to the Internet. The Internet was now ready for the revolution.

Developing separately from the Internet, the NSFNET backbone created a new network over which computers were able to communicate. In 1991 Tim Berner-Lee developed a new set of protocols, including 'http', URL, and 'html', separate from the Internet and designed to run on the NSFNET backbone. It was the development of these protocols that created the interface of today's World Wide Web. By 2004 the World Wide Web was growing 2 million annually and estimates have placed the current number of registered domains worldwide at over 40 million.

The year 1993 was marked by the development on the first mainstream web browser software Mosaic. The Web was now poised for the development of today's rich content that makes the Web so dynamic. The advent of the Web protocols and the browser enabled the World Wide Web to separate itself from the Internet according to the rich graphical interface that was now possible on the Web. Corporations now had a new and exciting medium to display their corporate messages as well as achieve a level of consumer interactivity that was never before possible.

It was not long after the advent of the Internet, and later the World Wide Web that network administrators began to fear that traffic was approaching self-destructive levels. The Internet was originally designed to handle the transfer of two articles per day between nodes and data traffic quickly began to push the limit of the new networks. The same year that Tim Berner-Lee developed the World Wide Web protocols, NSFNET upgraded the congested backbone to new T-3 bundled telephone lines. With the new backbone in place the Internet and the Web were now ready for the unprecedented growth witnessed in the mid 1990's to the present. The backbone was now in place to handle the individual dial-up access which has expanded the Internet and the World Wide Web from a handful of large corporations and researchers at various universities to the individual consumers, businesses, and computer enthusiasts.

Internet and World Wide Web Access

In 1990 "The World" became the first ever provider of commercial dial up access. This marked a huge turning point in the history of the Internet and the World Wide Web as these networks were now available to individuals and business. What had previously been accessible by only a handful of researchers and government agencies was now available to the world. This was one of the biggest steps in bringing the Internet and the World Wide Web to the forefront of business. Until individual consumers and businesses were able to access these networks there was no commercial value to the Internet and the Web. In 1995 several new dial up companies appeared and began providing access to the Internet and the World Wide Web. America Online and MSN quickly developed the infrastructure to bring the Internet and the Web to the masses. These companies positioned themselves as the telephone companies of the Internet and the World Wide Web. The rise of these Internet Service Providers and their ability to provide affordable access to the Internet and the Web has been one of the single biggest steps to the commercialization of these networks.

World Wide Web and Electronic Commerce

With the World Wide Web in the homes and businesses of tens of millions of people worldwide, businesses now have a new and exciting method of conveying their corporate messages. Companies began to shift resources away from traditional advertising methods and into Web campaigns. Forward-thinking companies were quick to take advantage of the unique advantages that the World Wide Web presented. Here was a totally revolutionary way for companies to achieve a level of interactivity and intimacy with consumers that marketers had never before dreamed possible. Additionally, instead of trying to capture the attention of potential consumers as with radio, Television, and newspaper advertisements, here was a system in which consumers were actually seeking out product/service information from the company.

Businesses were now able to present corporate information to consumers at the point of sale. Companies no longer had to sit and hope that consumers would follow an advertisement to the store. Consumers could now be exposed to an advertisement and then immediately make a purchase. Fortune 500 companies quickly began to compile web budgets and most were investing in information technology (IT) to get their web sites up and running. Many Fortune 500 companies have continued to spend as much as several hundred thousand dollars per year to maintain and market their web sites.

As the Web continued to grow, web sites began to move beyond just an on-line brochure. Companies quickly began to build not only sites with appealing graphical content and informative copy, but sites that implemented secured credit systems to accept on-line purchases and entire databases to compile consumer information and manage products on-line as well. This new point-of-purchase situation that was created as the World Wide Web continued to develop enabled sellers to generate revenue from additional sources. Manufacturers could now sell directly to consumers, smaller domestic companies could now sell internationally, and an entire niche of new businesses began to pop up seemingly daily. This new method of electronic commerce quickly enabled the Web to become an even more powerful business resource.

However, with the development of this new way to shop for and buy products came new challenges for businesses to overcome. First and foremost, how were consumers going to pay for their purchases? Secondly, with past experiences with individuals gaining uninvited access to computer networks, security issues began to be raised as it became apparent that large amounts of money would now be changing hands daily over this new network. Finally, businesses needed to address the subtle challenges that arose from e-commerce such as new methods for organizing products on-line and maximizing consumer convenience, as well as completely new marketing strategies and techniques.

As companies began to sell on the Internet in ever increasing sales volumes it became increasingly important to develop, or integrate, a monetary system that would be compatible with this new medium. A myriad of currency systems quickly popped up on the Web. However, it has been the integration of credit card processing via the Web that has come to dominate e-commerce transactions. As credit transactions over the Web became the preferred method for purchasing goods many of the initial on-line currency systems have vanished. However, there are still several alternatives to paying with credit cards that exist. These few, viable payment methods, while not as popular as credit transactions still remain an important means to giving consumers and sellers flexibility in e-commerce.

How The Internet Is Affecting Different Industries

The Internet is affecting all businesses in similar ways. Every industry, for example, has suddenly become part of a global network where all companies are equally easy to reach. However, even though the forces affecting them are the same, the consequences for each industry are very different.

Financial Services

Universal access to information is hitting hard in the financial services industry. This is a classic example of how the Internet can open up an existing infrastructure. In the past, brokers have justified their high fees by pointing to the quality of their advice, but now knowledgeable amateurs and industry experts can trade stock for no charge in popular personal investing sites such as the Motley Fool. Investors can get advice and market information from many sources other than full-service brokers, so they are less willing to pay a premium just to trade. The challenge here is to survive on thin margins, or find some way to add value.

The brokerage business adapted to the Internet faster than any other arm of finance. To make a trade, all you need to do is log on to the Web site of your online broker, and with a few keystrokes and a few clicks of your mouse to identify the stock and number of shares involved in the transaction, you can buy and sell securities in seconds. In addition, an overwhelming amount of free information is available to online investors—from the latest Securities & Exchange filings to the rumors spread in chat rooms.

Online banking customers can check balances of their savings, checking, and loan accounts; transfer money among accounts; and pay their bills. These customers enjoy the convenience of not writing checks in longhand, think they have a better knowledge of their current balances, and appreciate the reduction of expenditures on envelopes and stamps

Auctions

The Internet has created many new options for C2C e-commerce, including electronic auctions, in which geographically dispersed buyers and sellers can come together. A special type of auction called *bidding* allows a prospective buyer to place only one bid for an item or a service. Priceline.com's initial business model enabled consumers to achieve significant savings by naming their own price for goods and services. Pnceline.com took these consumer offers and then presented them to sellers, who filled as much of the demand as they wished at price points determined by the buyers.

eBay selected Pitney Bowes to provide its postage service, which gives its customers easy access to U.S. Postal Service (USPS) shipping services. With this new tool, eBay users can purchase postage online, pay for it using their PayPal accounts, and print their shipping label from their computer—all from the eBay Web site. Once the label is purchased, both the buyer and the seller will be able to track the delivery status of the package online from the eBay site. Simplifying the shipping part of the transaction will make trading on eBay faster and easier.

Retailing

E-commerce is being used extensively in retailing and wholesaling. Electronic retailing, sometimes called *e-tailing*, is the direct sale of products or services by businesses to consumers through electronic storefronts, which are typically designed around the familiar electronic catalog and shopping cart model. Companies such as Office Depot, Wal-Mart, and many others have used the same model to sell wholesale to employees of corporations. There are tens of thousands of electronic retail Web sites—selling literally everything from soup to nuts. In addition, cybermalls are another means to support retail shopping. A cybermall is a single Web site that offers many products and services at one Internet location—similar to a regular shopping mall. An Internet cybermall pulls multiple buyers and sellers into one virtual place, easily reachable through a Web browser. For example, PC Mall is a hardware, software, and consumer electronics retailer that sells items for the home, garden, and office decor; patriotic merchandise; gifts, collectibles, toys, and games; electronics; travel accessories; business supplies; sporting goods; tools and home hardware; health and beauty products; jewelry; and more.

A key sector of wholesale e-commerce is spending on manufacturing, repair, and operations (MRO) goods and services—from simple office supplies to mission-critical equipment, such as the motors, pumps, compressors, and instruments that keep manufacturing facilities up and running smoothly. MRO purchases often approach 40 percent of a manufacturing company's total revenues, but the purchasing system can be haphazard, without automated controls. In addition to these external purchase costs, companies face significant internal costs resulting from outdated and cumbersome MRO management processes. For example, studies show that a high percentage of manufacturing downtime often results from not having the right part at the right time in the right place. The result is lost productivity and capacity. E-commerce software for plant operations provides powerful comparative searching capabilities to enable managers to identify functionally equivalent items, helping them spot opportunities to combine purchases for cost savings. Comparing various suppliers, coupled with consolidating more spending with fewer suppliers, leads to decreased costs. In addition, automated workflows are typically based on industry best practices, which can streamline processes.

Manufacturing

One approach taken by many manufacturers to raise profitability and improve customer service is to move their supply chain operations onto the Internet. Here they can form an electronic exchange to join with competitors and suppliers alike, using computers and Web sites to buy and sell goods, trade market information, and run back-office operations, such as inventory control. With such an exchange, the business center is not a physical building but a network-based location where business interactions occur. This approach has greatly speeded up the movement of raw materials and finished products among all members of the business community, thus reducing the amount of inventory that must be maintained. It has also led to a much more competitive marketplace and lower prices. Private exchanges are owned and operated by a single company. The owner uses the exchange to trade exclusively with established business partners. Public exchanges are owned and operated by industry groups. They provide services and a common technology platform to their members and are open, usually for a fee, to any company that wants to use them.

One example of a successful exchange is the WorldWide Retail Exchange (WWRE) founded in 2000 by 17 international retailers to enable participants in the food, general merchandise, textile/home, and drugstore sectors to simplify and automate supply chain processes.

Advertising and Marketing

The nature of the Web allows firms to gather much more information about customer behavior and preferences than they could using other marketing approaches. Marketing organizations can measure many online activities as customers and potential customers gather information and make their purchase decisions. Analysis of this data is complicated because of the Web's interactivity and because each visitor voluntarily provides or refuses to provide personal data such as name, address, e-mail address, telephone number, and demographic data. Internet advertisers use the data they gather to identify specific portions of their markets and target them with tailored advertising messages. This practice, called market segmentation, divides the pool of potential customers into subgroups, which are usually defined in terms of demographic characteristics such as age, gender, marital status, income level, and geographic location.

Technology-enabled relationship management is a new twist on establishing direct customer relationships made possible when firms promote and sell on the Web. Technology-enabled relationship management occurs when a firm obtains detailed information about a customer's behavior, preferences, needs, and buying patterns and uses that information to set prices, negotiate terms, tailor promotions, add product features, and otherwise customize its entire relationship with that customer. DoubleClick is a leading global Internet advertising company that leverages technology and media expertise to help advertisers use the power of the Web to build relationships with customers.

Exhibit 3.1 lists some prominent examples of the digital economy

Exhibit 3.1: The Digital Economy

Computer software
Movies
Books
Music albums
Financial transactions
Video conferencing
Educational and training materials
E-mail
Information services
Bulletin boards and chat rooms
Telecommunications
Internet access services
Magazines
Electronic bill payments
Stock trading
Newspapers

Games
Business databases
Remote medical diagnosis
Remote repairs
Home banking

E-commerce is now revolutionizing both business-to-business and business-to-consumer sales by introducing a number of new business models for connecting suppliers and consumers. These models include on-line catalogs, virtual communities, portals, auctions, reverse auctions, subscription—based services, infomediaries, and aggregators (see Exhibit 3.2).

Exhibit 3.2: e-Commerce Business Models

On-Line Catalogs:	Sites where ".com" retailers such as Amazon.com sell their products.
Virtual Communities:	Sites that connect a targeted demographic, such as iVillage's focus on women.
Portals:	Sites such as Lycos or Yahoo! that offer a variety of services such as calendar, news, E-mail, search engines, content, and shopping malls.
Auctions:	Sites such as eBay that allow thousands of individuals and businesses to sell goods or services to the highest bidder.
Reverse Auctions:	Sites such as priceline.com where buyers can name the price they are willing to pay for goods and services and try to be matched with a seller of such goods or services.
Subscription-Based Services:	Sites such as CCH on-line where information or some other product is sold based on a monthly subscription payment.
Infomediaries:	Sites such as Autobytel that provide specialized or industry-specific information on product quality, prices, financing, and so on, on behalf of producers of goods and services and their potential customers.
Aggregators:	Sites such as Accompany where either buyers or sellers combine to increase their market power.

41

Advantages of Electronic Commerce

Firms are interested in electronic commerce because, quite simply, it can help increase profits. All the advantages of electronic commerce for businesses can be summarized in one statement: Electronic commerce can increase sales and decrease costs. E-commerce will offer the buyers increased selection, convenience, and better deals. Advertising done well on the Web can get even a small firm's promotional message out to potential customers in every country in the world. A firm can use electronic commerce to reach narrow market segments that are geographically scattered. The Web is particularly useful in creating virtual communities that become ideal target markets for specific types of products or services. A virtual community is a gathering of people who share a common interest, but instead of this gathering occurring in the physical world; it takes place on the Internet.

> - A business can reduce the costs of handling sales inquiries, providing price quotes, and determining product availability by using electronic commerce in its sales support and order-taking processes.
> - Electronic commerce provides buyers with a wider range of choices than traditional commerce.
> - Electronic commerce provides buyers with an easy way to customize the level of detail in the information they obtain about a prospective purchase.
> - Electronic payments of tax refunds, public retirement, and welfare support cost less to issue and arrive securely and quickly when transmitted over the Internet.
> - Electronic payments can be easier to audit and monitor than payments made by check, providing protection against fraud and theft losses.
> - Electronic commerce can also make products and services available in remote areas.
> - Electronic commerce is a great way to get the business of these "off-peak" shoppers. A company can put a web site up for a very small amount of money and have their "cyber-shop" open 24 hours a day and 7 days a week.

Disadvantages of Electronic Commerce

Some business processes may never lend themselves to electronic commerce. For example, perishable foods and high-cost, unique items, such as custom-designed jewelry and antiques, may be impossible to inspect adequately from a remote location, regardless of any technologies that might be devised in the future. Most of the disadvantages of electronic commerce today, however, stem from the newness and rapidly developing pace of the underlying technologies. These disadvantages will disappear as electronic commerce matures and becomes more available to and accepted by the general population.

Disadvantages include:

▷ Return-on-investment is difficult to calculate.

▷ Many firms have had trouble recruiting and retaining employees with the technological, design, and business process skills needed to create an effective electronic commerce presence.

▷ Difficulty of integrating existing databases and transaction-processing software designed for traditional commerce into the software that enables electronic commerce.

▷ Many businesses face cultural and legal obstacles to conducting electronic commerce.

E-commerce Strategy

Successful E-commerce business strategies must address an entirely new set of challenges unique to the World Wide Web. As with all new business ventures intense research is vital to the success of e-commerce systems. Research will not only uncover what it takes to get started, but will also expose potential markets. The Internet has been thought of as the perfect environment for 'niche' projects. Because of the access the World Wide Web offers to potential consumers across various geographic and demographic sectors niche e-commerce systems have been particularly successful. While it is not necessarily a prerequisite for e-commerce, developing a niche market will give any potential e-commerce project an immediate advantage.

In addition to uncovering certain niche markets, research will also provide potential Web entrepreneurs with the information to implement the proper systems required for successful e-commerce. These systems include encryption of transmissions, shopping cart or product database features, and types of payment to accept. Implementing the proper, convenient product management systems as well as encrypting any confidential transactions will result in increased sales. Likewise it is important to choose the best method for purchasing products. It is recommended that any e-commerce purchasing system be based on credit card transactions.

With the appropriate back-end systems in place, it is crucial that any successful e-commerce site provide a good HTML interface to the consumer. Appearances on the World Wide Web are very important. With many niche e-commerce sites, the appearance of the web site will be the first contact a business will have with a consumer. Because of this fact it is exceedingly important that e-commerce sites provide a good HTML interface. This HTML interface is what makes the first impression to the consumer. The appearance of successful e-commerce web sites will belie a clean, professional appearance that is easy to read and move through.

While a good HTML interface is crucial it may be completely ineffective if consumers are not coming to an e-commerce site. To overcome this, successful e-commerce systems will take an aggressive, tireless approach to marketing the e-commerce site. Search engine listing and relisting, conducting banner and link exchanges, issuance of press releases, and mass electronic mail campaigns will generate the exposure that is vital to the success of the e-commerce site. Additional value-added content features such as pre- and post-sales support, testimonials, and personalized customer support should be included in any e-commerce web site. Other features including multi-lingual capabilities, contests, multiple methods for ordering (i.e. via facsimile or 800 numbers) will only increase sales. It is especially important to allow consumers to order multiple ways as many consumers are still leery of providing credit information over the Web. The providing of multiple methods for ordering will allow sellers to receive orders from consumers who would not have otherwise made a purchase over the Web.

On-Line Security

With personal credit information being transferred across networks as well as other confidential information, security has always been a major concern of both businesses and consumers. To provide a viable e-commerce system businesses must address the issue of security. Businesses now protect themselves and their consumers by encrypting transmissions of credit information and other confidential data. Secure Server Lockout system, as well as firewall systems to protect on-line accounting, billing, and product management and electronic mail databases help provide the encryption necessary to protect the seller and the consumer. In order to insure secured transmissions e-commerce systems must obtain secure certification from the site host to publicize that site as secure.

While e-commerce sites design systems to protect themselves and their consumers, consumers may take an active role in insuring the security of their transmissions. *ZDNet On-line Magazine* urges consumers to only buy from secured sites, and educate themselves on an e-commerce site's privacy policies. Watchdog organizations such as the "Trustee" have been formed to police the privacy policies of e-commerce sites for consumers. Consumers should provide only that information required to process the order, and to always order with credit cards. Ordering via credit card, as opposed to alternative payment methods, provides an extra layer of security as credit card companies will reimburse consumers for fraud perpetrated by e-commerce merchants. Finally, the Office of the United States Attorney General recommends that consumers use an 800- number to place orders whenever possible. Finally, consumers may educate themselves on the various on-line scams through the non-profit groups such as the US Consumer Gateway, the FTC, and the Internet Fraud Watch.

Web 2.0

Amazon.com was one of the first to recognize other possibilities when it added the "Customers Who Bought This Book Also Bought" feature to its Web site. That idea was the first step toward what has come to be known as Web 2.0. The term "Web 2.0" describes the changing trends in the use of World Wide Web technology and web design that aim to enhance creativity, communications, secure information sharing, collaboration and functionality of the web. Web 2.0 concepts have led to the development and evolution of web culture communities and hosted services, such as social-networking sites, video sharing sites, wikis, and blogs. Exhibit 3.3 compares Web 2.0 to traditional processing. (For some reason, the term Web 1.0 is not used.)

Exhibit 3.3: Comparison of Traditional Processing with Web 2.0

Traditional Processing	Web 2.0 Processing
Software as product	Software as service
Infrequent, controlled releases	Frequent releases of perpetual betas
Business model relies on sale of software licenses	Business model relies on advertising or other revenue from use
Extensive advertising	Viral marketing
Product value fixed	Product value increases with use and users
Controlled, fixed interface	Organic interfaces, mashups encouraged
Publishing	Participation
All rights reserved	Some rights reserved
Major winners: Microsoft, Oracle, SAP	Major winners: Google, Amazon.com, eBay

Software as a Service

Google, Amazon.com, and eBay exemplify Web 2.0. These companies do not sell software licenses, because software is not their product. Instead, they provide **software as a service.** You can search Google, run Google Docs & Spreadsheets, use Google Earth, process Gmail, and access Google maps—all from a thin-client program in your browser, with the bulk of the processing occurring on a Google server, somewhere on the Internet. Google releases new versions of its programs, like all of those in Web 2.0, frequently. Instead of software license fees, the Web 2.0 business model relies on advertising or other revenue that results as users employ the software as a service.

Many Web 2.0 programs are perpetually classified as "beta." Traditionally, a **beta** program is a prerelease version of software that is used for testing; it becomes obsolete when the final version is released. In the Web 2.0 world, many programs are always beta. Features and functions are constantly changing; none of the functions listed in the *More* menu item existed 2 years ago. But, because the program remains classified as beta, with no license fee, no user can complain about the changing user interface.

Traditional software vendors depend on software license fees. If many Office users switched to word processors and spreadsheets provided as software as a service, the hit on Microsoft revenue would be catastrophic. Because of the importance of software license revenue, substantial marketing efforts are made to convert users to new releases.

In the Web 2.0 world, no such marketing is done; new features are released and vendors wait for users to spread the news to one another, in what is called **viral marketing.** Google has never announced, in a formal marketing campaign, any software. Users carry the message to one another. In fact, if a product requires advertising to be successful, then it is not a Web 2.0 product.

Use Increases Value

Another characteristic of Web 2.0 is that the value of the site increases with users and use. Amazon.com gains more value as more users write more reviews. Amazon.com becomes *the* place to go for information about books or other products. Similarly, the more people who buy or sell on eBay, the more eBay gains value as a site.

Contrast this with traditional products where the value is fixed. Millions upon millions of Microsoft Word users may have created templates of potential use to others, but because Microsoft does not serve as a clearinghouse for sharing those templates the value of Word does not grow with the number of Word users.

Organic User Interface and Mashups

The traditional software model carefully controls the users' experience. All Office programs share a common user interface; the ribbon (toolbar) in Word is similar to the ribbon in PowerPoint and in Excel. In contrast, Web 2.0 interfaces are organic. Users find their way around eBay and PayPal, and if the user interface changes from day to day, well, that is just the nature of Web 2.0. Further, Web 2.0 encourages **mashups,** *which occur when the output from two or more Web sites is combined into a single user experience.*

Google's My Maps is an excellent mashup example. Google publishes Google Maps (created, incidentally, by a vendor other than Google) and provides tools for users to make custom modifications to those maps. Thus, users mash the Google map product with their own knowledge. Users share their experiences or photos of hiking trips or other travel.

Participation and Ownership Differences

Mashups lead to another key difference. Traditional sites are about publishing; Web 2.0 is about participation. Users provide reviews, map content, discussion responses, blog entries, and so forth. A final difference, listed in Exhibit 3.3, concerns *ownership*. Traditional vendors and Web sites lock down all the legal rights they can. For example, Oracle publishes content and demands that others obtain written permission before reusing it. Web 2.0 locks down only some rights. Google publishes maps and says, "Do what you want with them. We'll help you share them."

E-commerce and the Future

On the seller side of e-commerce, declining web development costs, advanced security, better product management, and inventory, sales, and accounting systems integration will pull more businesses to e-commerce into the future. As businesses continue to enjoy increasing success through their e-commerce sites, it will become increasing important for competitors to develop some level of e-commerce or they will lose market share. In fact, e-commerce has become so important to today's business world that companies that have been slow to adopt some level of e-commerce have suffered lagging stock performance on Wall Street. Market analysts are demanding to know what plans companies are making for incorporating e-commerce systems. From a consumer standpoint dramatically increased connection speeds will make buying on the Web increasingly attractive. E-commerce will continue to offer consumers increased selection, convenience, and in many cases better deals as it is easier than ever for manufacturers to sell directly to the consumer thus eliminating the costs of wholesalers and retailers. Wireless and hand-held devices such as iPhone will be a new avenue for E-commerce.

Electronic Data Interchange (EDI) is a standard for exchanging documents from machine to machine, electronically. Another alternative is eXtensible Markup Language (XML), a standard markup language that offers advantages over EDI and that most believe will eventually replace EDI.

Summary

As business moves into the next millennium, and e-commerce becomes a multi-trillion dollar economy, more operations and traditional business software platforms will become integrated into a Web platform. Advances in connectivity and the downward trend in computer prices will bring more people worldwide onto the Internet and the Web. In the next millennium, E-commerce may become the way that international business is conducted. A global economy developed over the World Wide Web

CHAPTER 4

Intranet and Extranet

Intranet utilization in corporate America is rapidly growing. Because Intranets use Internet technology, there is ready access to external data. In effect, Intranets are internal Web sites. An Intranet is an important tool to use in business and is developed and used by the company itself.

An Intranet is easy to install and flexible (what is developed for one platform may be used for others). A secure network that uses the Internet as its main backbone network to connect the intranets of a company's different locations, or to establish extranet links between a company and its customers, suppliers, and other business partners is called a Virtual private Network (VPN).

Corporate managers must have knowledge of Intranet structure and organization because it relates to accounting, tax, audit, control, and security issues. Managers, customers, employees, stockholders, potential investors, creditors, loan officers, government agent representatives (SEC, IRS), and other interested parties can access the database or information in a company through Web browsers (interfaces) such as Netscape Navigator and Microsoft's Internet Explorer. Management may set up an Intranet to improve operating efficiencies and productivity and to reduce operating costs (e.g., distribution expenses), time, and errors. Of course, keeping information on the Intranet current takes time and resources. Proper controls must be established to guard against unauthorized access of the company's data through the Internet. One security device is the use of firewalls (barriers) to protect the company's Intranet by unauthorized access, and to prevent misuse of the Intranet by outsiders who might otherwise be able to alter accounting and financial information, steal property, obtain confidential data, or commit other inappropriate or fraudulent acts. Further, add-on security tools are available to restrict users by preventing them from performing certain acts, or from viewing certain "restricted" information.

In an Intranet, one protocol connects all users to the Web server, run on standard protocols supported by any computer.

Intranet Explosion

Information System (IS) and functional department managers quickly saw the power of this new communications medium as a resource to be leveraged on the corporate network. Forrester Research did a study finding that two-thirds of large companies already had or are contemplating some use of Intranet business applications. Surveyed companies identified the Intranet as a powerful tool to make information more readily available within and outside the company.

With businesses under significant pressure to empower employees and to better leverage internal information resources, Intranets furnish a very effective communications platform, one that is both timely and extensive. A basic Intranet can be set up in days and can eventually act as an "information hub" for the whole company, its remote offices, partners, suppliers, customers, investors, creditors, consultants, regulatory agencies, and other interested parties.

Intranets provide the following features:
- Easy navigation (internal home page provides links to information)
- Can integrate distributed computing strategy (localized web sewers residing near the content author)
- Rapid prototyping (can be measured in days or even hours in some cases)
- Accessible via most computing platforms
- Scaleable (start small, build as requirements dictate)
- Extensible to many media types (video, audio, interactive applications)
- Can be tied in to "legacy" information sources (databases, existing word processing documents, groupware databases)

The benefits to these features are many, including:
- An Intranet is inexpensive to start, requires minimal investment in dollars or infrastructure.
- Open platform architecture means large (and increasing) numbers of add-on applications.
- A distributed computing strategy uses computing resources more effectively.
- An Intranet is much more timely and less expensive than traditional information (paper) delivery.

Calendar-Driven Versus Event-Driven Strategy

One of the key drivers in the Intranet adoption curve is they allow businesses to evolve from a "calendar" or "schedule" based publishing strategy, to one of an "event-driven" or "needs-based" publishing strategy. In the past, businesses published an employee handbook once a year, whether or not policies changed to coincide with that publication date. Traditionally, even though these handbooks may have been outdated as soon as they arrived on the users' desks (and were promptly misplaced), they would not be updated until next year.

With an Intranet publishing strategy, information can be updated instantly. If the company adds a new mutual fund to the 401K program, content on the benefits page can be immediately updated to incorporate that change, and the company internal home page can have a brief announcement about the change. Then when employees refer to the 401K program, they have the new information at their fingertips. Content can be changed or updated to reflect new rules at any time.

Intranets Reduce Cost, Time To Market

Intranets dramatically reduce the costs (and time) of content development, duplication, distribution, and usage. The traditional publication model includes a multistep process including creation of content, migration of content to desktop publishing environment, production of draft, revision, final draft production, duplication, and distribution.

The Intranet publishing model includes a much shorter process, skipping many of the steps involved in the traditional publication model. In the Intranet model, revision becomes part of the updating process while the original content is available to end users, thus dramatically reducing the time it takes for the information to become available to the user. As the information is centrally stored and always presumed to be current, the company will not have to retrieve "old" information from employees, thus saving updating expenses.

This new publishing model significantly reduces both costs and the time frame. Assuming that the corporate Local Area Network (LAN) environment can support Intranet activities (and most can), the Information Technology (IT) infrastructure is already in place. Further, most popular Intranet web servers can run on platforms widely found in most companies (Intel Pentium class computers, Apple Macintosh, Novell NetWare, etc.), so that little if any additional infrastructure is required.

Organizations estimate that the traditional model may entail physical duplication and distribution costs of as high as $15 per employee, costs separate from the content development or testing phases. An organization with 10,000 employees may find potential cost savings of moving to an Intranet policy for a single application alone --the employee policies and benefits manual--of $150,000. This cost savings does not even consider the additional value in an Intranet solution which makes information more easily available to staff, thus improving their productivity and morale.

Practical Applications

The uses of Intranets (internal Webs) by companies are unlimited, including:
   ▷ Furnishing outside CPAs with accounting, audit, and tax information.

- Providing marketing and sales information to current and prospective customers or clients.
- Providing information to salespersons in the field and managers at different branches (e.g., sales and profit reports, product tracking, transaction analysis).
- Furnishing resource needs and reports to suppliers.
- Communicating corporate information to employees, such as company policies and forms, operating instructions, job descriptions, time sheets, human resource data and documents, business plans, newsletters, marketing manuals, phone directories, schedules, and performance reports.
- Assisting in employee training, development, and technical support.
- Transferring information to government agencies (e.g., Department of Commerce, SEC, IRS).
- Furnishing current and prospective investors with profitability, growth, and market value statistics.
- Providing lenders and creditors with useful liquidity and solvency data.
- Providing project, proposal, and scheduling data to participating companies in joint ventures.
- Providing press releases and product/service announcements.
- Giving legal information to outside attorneys in litigation matters.
- Providing trade associations with input for their surveys.
- Accessing and searching databases and rearranging information.
- Furnishing information to outside consultants (e.g., investment management advisors, pension planners).
- Providing insurance companies with information to draft or modify insurance coverage.
- Allowing for collaborative workgroups such as letting users access various drafts of a specific project document interactively and adding annotations and comments. For example, Ford's Intranet links design engineers in the U.S., Europe, and Asia.
- Furnishing economic statistics about the company to economic advisors.
- Facilitating database queries and document requests.
- Providing spreadsheets, database reports, tables, checklists, and graphs to interested parties.
- Displaying e-mail.

Site maps (e.g., Table of Contents) should be included so users may easily navigate from each note (element) and are visible through frames or panels.

An Intranet requires Web application development for its internal network such as appropriate Web servers. For quick response time, there should be a direct connection to the server. Web browsers may be used to achieve cross-platform viewing and applications for a wide variety of desktops used within the company. The use of Web technology (e.g., Web servers) allows each desktop having a Web browser to access corporate information over the existing network. Therefore, employees in different divisions of the company located in different geographic areas (e.g., buildings) can access and use centralized and/or scattered information (cross section).

There are many client/server applications within and among companies such as cross-platform applications. The major element in an Intranet is the Web server software which runs on a central computer and serves as a clearinghouse for all information. Web servers for the Intranet are available from many vendors including:

▶ IBM (800-426-2255). Internet Connection Server for MVS.
▶ Microsoft (800-426-9400). Internet Information Server (comes with Microsoft's NT Server).
▶ Netscape (415-528-2555). Fast Track and Commerce Server for Windows NT.

There are many Intranet tool vendors such as Spider Technologies www.spider.com. For example, Spider Technologies' Intranet Genie is an Intranet tool, which includes a fairly secure Web server, HTML authoring instructions and guidelines (discussed below), Web browser, and e-mail functions. Regardless of the operating system (e.g., Windows, UNIX, Macintosh), many Intranet tools are available.

Hypertext Markup Language(HTML)

The Hypertext Markup Language (HTML) should be used in developing Intranets because it is an easier Graphical User Interface (GUI) to program than windows environments such as Motif or Microsoft Windows. HTML is a good integrating tool for database applications and information systems. It facilitates the use of hyper links and search engines enabling the easy sharing of identical information among different responsibility segments of the company. Intranet data usually goes from back-end sources (e.g., mainframe host) to the Web server to users (e.g., customers) in HTML format.

Common Gateway Interface (CGI)

The majority of Web applications run through a mechanism in the Web server referred to as the common gateway interface (CGI). CGI is used to connect users to databases. Most CGI programs are written in TCL or Pert (a scripting language). However, due to the fact that these languages involve printing a source code of the Web server, there is an unsecured situation from a control and security standpoint. Other deficiencies are relative slowness in applications, nonexistence or inadequate debuggers, and maintenance problems. Consider other languages for the CGI such as C or C++.

The following CGI business applications are recommended:

▶ In developing Web applications for INTRANETS, code management tools are needed to enable different participants in a corporate project or activity to communicate and work together. You must also use tools for database design, modeling, and debugging.

▶ Do not commit to a particular server or browser because new technological developments require flexibility. Set up your system so that it may accommodate many servers and browsers.

▶ Make sure your HTML user interface is separate from the database and application logic.

Setting up an Intranet

Intranet applications are scaleable--they can start small and grow. This feature allows many businesses to "try out" an Intranet pilot--to publish a limited amount of content on a single platform, and evaluate the results. If the pilot looks promising, additional content can be migrated to the Intranet server.

Proposed Content

Companies must ascertain if data should be made available via a web server, via e-mail, or by some other means. If the data is of general import, such as company travel guidelines or mileage reimbursement, it can be posted on a web server so that when employees and travel agents, among others, require this information, they click on Travel Guidelines from the human resources page, and obtain the most current information.

Many businesses find building web interfaces to "legacy information" a key application. With tools such as Purveyor's Data Wizard, HTML Transit, and WebDBC, end users can build simple point and click access to this legacy information without any programming, making it available to nontechnical users through their web browser. Key database applications include: customer records, product information, inventory, technical problem tracking, call reports, etc. In addition, individuals can quickly set up seminar or training registration forms for short-term usage, loading the registrants' information into an easily manipulated database.

Conversely, interoffice e-mail may be more appropriate for "interrupt-driven" time sensitive information, especially for a focused group of recipients." Our most important customer is coming in March 2, so please attend the briefing at 9 A.M." In this case, the web server can be used as an extended information resource: "Before the meeting, check the internal web server link for Current Customers for updated information concerning this account."

Enhancements

Intranets can provide efficient access to other external information resources including group access to mailing lists, threaded discussion groups, and stock/bond quotes. In this way, the oft-accessed information can be aggregated at the firewall and efficiently dispersed within the company, thus reducing external bandwidth and connectivity requirements.

Multithreaded discussion group software, or conferencing applications, can run on the same platform as the Intranet application, providing further chances to discuss company issues and the content that resides on the server.

Intranets Compared to Groupware

Intranets and groupware are not mutually exclusive. Many companies find that groupware (work flow, collaborative computing, etc.) is appropriate for certain focused applications, while Intranets are suitable for migrating existing content to online delivery. Others find a powerful combination in groupware and a web server (Lotus InterNotes engine for publishing Notes databases on the web, for example).

Ultimately, each application strategy has its merits. Beyond this, Intranet applications and web servers make an excellent foundation for web-based groupware, allowing businesses to employ a web-centric Intranet system strategy and leverage the nearly ubiquitous web browser and the powerful navigational aids provided by HTML.

The Business Value of Intranets

Studies have shown that early adopters of intranets have been provided with impressive returns and high paybacks at low costs. Many corporate intranet users and consultants to the global business community have suggested that companies should get going fast on pilot intranet projects, or quickly expand any current intranet initiatives.

Communications and Collaboration

Intranets can significantly improve communications and collaboration within an enterprise. Examples include:
- ▷ Using an intranet browser and PC or NC workstation to send and receive E-mail, voicemail, paging, and faxes to communicate with others within your organization, and externally through the Internet and extranets.
- ▷ Using intranet groupware features to improve team and project collaboration with services such as discussion groups, chat rooms, and audio and videoconferencing.

Web Publishing

The advantages of developing and publishing hyperlinked multimedia documents to hypermedia databases accessible on World Wide Web servers has moved to corporate intranets. The comparative ease, attractiveness, and lower cost of publishing and accessing multimedia business information internally via intranet websites has been one of the primary reasons for the explosive growth in the use of intranets in business. Examples include:

- ▶ Company newsletters, technical drawings, and product catalogs can be published in a variety of ways including hypermedia and Web pages, E-mail, net broadcasting, and as part of in-house business applications.
- ▶ Intranet software browsers, servers, and search engines can help you easily navigate and locate the business information you need.

Business Operations and Management

Intranets are being used as the platform for developing and deploying critical business applications to support business operations and managerial decision making across the internetworked enterprise. Employees within the company, or external business partners can access and run such applications using Web browsers from anywhere on the network whenever needed. Examples include:

- ▶ Many companies are developing customer applications like order processing, inventory control, sales management, and executive information systems that can be implemented on intranets, extranets, and the Internet.
- ▶ Many applications are designed to interface with, and access, existing company databases and legacy systems. The software for such business uses (sometimes-called applets or crossware) is then installed on intranet Web servers.
- ▶ Employees within a company, or external business partners, can access and run applications using Web browsers from anywhere on the network whenever needed.

Intranets and Corporate Finance

The use of Intranets should be used for corporate real-time decision support. The true competitiveness of a firm is determined by the ability of its management to make accurate, timely decisions that improve profitability and long-term prospects. To make these decisions, an organization must possess knowledge about various customers, products, and suppliers, the availability of assets, the status of commitments, and the profitability of activities.

While most companies have sophisticated transaction systems that collect operational data, the information that managers require for decision making and performance measurement purposes is not readily available. The challenge remains in how tremendous amounts of corporate financial data will be transformed into useful information. The problem is that there is too much data and not enough meaningful information. Firms need to access certain information with which to make smart decisions without the clutter of data. Why? Because developing a response to an emerging business situation means sifting through large amounts of data from business units or product lines. To enable large-scale data analysis, firms are increasingly using online analytical processing (OLAP).

The problem is not limited to tools for analyzing the data. Accuracy, timeliness, and accessibility of the data are also important. With management facing increasing pressure to make profitable decisions faster, they need to be free of the constraints of time and space to access distributed data from their office, home, or the road, at all hours of the day (and night). The next generation of Intranet applications will be required to provide access to the full range of corporate data to make strategic decisions. This might involve developing software "intelligent agents" that pull together information from a variety of relational and legacy systems at regular intervals to construct an integrated view of business activities. These agents then transform the data into a consistent, easily accessible format and distribute it where needed for decision making. (see Exhibit 4.1).

Exhibit 4.1: Distributed computing environment

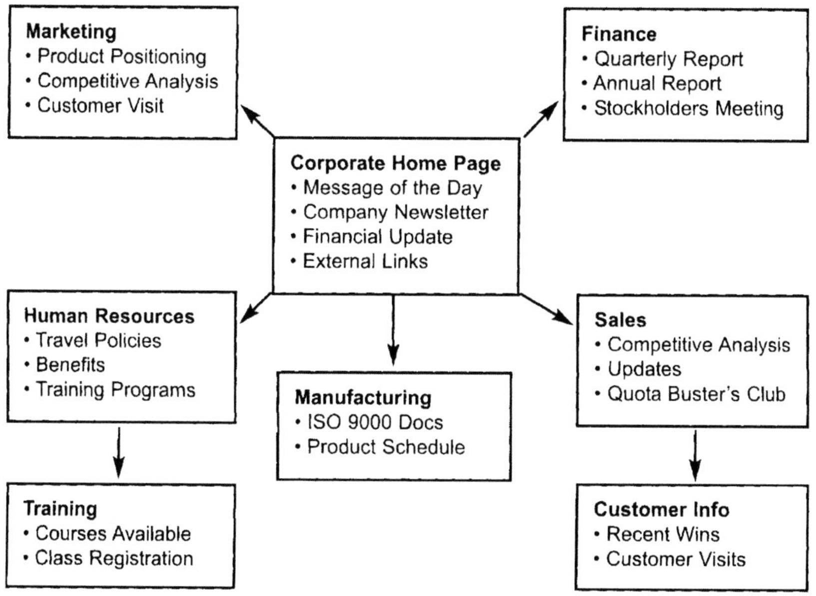

This section looks into the role of Intranets in financial management and how it can allow companies to deal with all their financial information, and what role it plays in the financial information management process.

Summarized here are the business problems faced, their solution, and their benefits after the solution is applied:

Business Problems:

▶ Non-integrated islands of valuable information
▶ Non-integrated financial and accounting applications
▶ Need for analysis tools and decision support for management

Solution:

▶ Fully integrated Web-based enterprise-wide financial and accounting infrastructure
▶ Benefits:
▶ Integrated information across business functions
▶ Improved data analysis and decision support
▶ Cost savings from increased efficiency

The competitive business environment is forcing firms to reengineer financial management processes. General ledger systems and spreadsheets alone prove inadequate when data is voluminous and worldwide, when corporate structures change because of mergers and acquisitions, and when timely and reliable consolidations, budgets, and forecasts are essential.

A definition of exactly what financial systems is required to establish the setting. Financial systems encompass business processes, procedures, controls, and data dedicated to the operation and maintenance of corporate financial objectives. It incorporates reporting and analyzing financial data, simplifying the budgeting and forecasting process, enabling better planning and controlling of the financial consolidation of actual results, answering *ad hoc* requests efficiently, and improving cost control and performance measurement. Financial systems are often triggered by events facing financial consequences such as receipt of appropriations or other financial resources, acquisition of goods or services, payments or collections, recognition of guarantees, benefits to be provided, potential liabilities, or other reportable financial activities. In technical aspects, financial systems usually have the following characteristics: a common database, common data element definitions, and standardized processing for transactions. A financial system includes multiple applications that are integrated through a common database or are interfaced to meet defined data and processing requirements.

For software developers to succeed in understanding the new business requirements that are emerging, in terms of functionality rather than technical architecture, they need to address the business issues and requirements, and not conversely. A review of what financial and accounting systems set out to do is in order. Accounting captures a firm's financial data, records and aggregates them, and statements are prepared that communicate to decision maker's necessary information about business units, transactions, and events. The early accounting system processed transactions, stored historical information, and used that information to answer questions about the past, present, and future. Today's accounting systems are a collection of methods for capturing and transforming financial data. An important aspect about accounting is to report the financial position of the firm and the performance of various business units to facilitate decision making. The accounting system is usually broken up into two types: financial and management accounting. Financial accounting collects, classifies, and reports financially based transactions subject to numerous disclosure requirements. The reports are used by external sources such as shareholders, investors, creditors, financial analysts, and the IRS. Financial accounting activities in the report include collecting, processing, maintaining, transmitting, and reporting data about financial events; supporting financial planning or budgeting activities, and supporting the preparation of financial statements.

Management accounting provides a financial analysis of management decisions and activities. The reports generated by the management accounting system are used by organizations internally. These reports prepare the report card by which operations managers are evaluated. Compared to financial accounting, management accounting is fairly new, having evolved from simple cost accounting systems. Management accounting activities include reporting historical transactions to internal and external parties, accumulating and reporting cost information, safeguarding the assets of a company, and providing insight with respects to the value of future transactions.

Financial Intranets

Finance and accounting software have typically been characterized as dull and not trendsetting. Accounting software, for instance, provided a way to enter transactions and manage those transactions in the form of an audit trail. The primary focus of accounting software was transaction entry and back office management of the audit trail, critically important but not very exciting.

Today there is a lot more that business managers need from the information locked inside accounting databases. In short, the information is there but it is very difficult to obtain. Intranets can play a big role in solving this problem because they will allow the integration necessary to provide accounting information that managers need, in the specific form they need it, when they need it, and where they need it.

Well managed companies watch their financial records carefully and set clear objectives for their managers. Providing access to important financial information securely and in an easy-to-use, online manner is a top priority. By using internal Web applications, finance departments can more easily disseminate this information to key managers by securely "posting" corporate finance information or by providing simple forms-based query capabilities. This will allow information to take the form of hundreds of specific views rather than one general view or report, like the typical set of financial statements.

New systems technologies offer integration and make it possible for information to be put into a system once and moved to all the different places. This frees accountants from having to spend time manually moving information from one place to another because there was no other way to accomplish the task. Accountants need to recognize the inevitable changes technology is going to bring about and must look for new ways to add value to the business. This value must be in alignment with the needs of the business process.

Finally, large financial systems developed in the era of mainframes have become too costly to maintain, troublesome to document, inefficient, ineffective, or even strategically dangerous as they are difficult to change as business conditions evolve.

The Purpose of Financial Intranets

Successful Intranet implementations should help tackle four problems that existing systems are not equipped to handle: production control, the effect on short-term and long-term strategy from daily operations, cost control, and the lack of control over report generating.

With the increasing amount of global sourcing, financial flows related to production are becoming more complicated. Currently, managers rely on a patchwork of systems to support financial management activities, such as accounts payable, accounts receivable, fixed-asset management, purchasing, and general ledger. These systems worked well when their primary responsibility was to collect and present historical information. Not surprisingly, most of these systems are only equipped to handle routine transactions, and little consideration is given to their connection to other business activities. For example, if the general ledger and the procurement systems were linked through an integrated information process, the financial analyst would have an accurate picture of accounts payable. By integrating financial functions into decision making, the organization can assess the financial consequences of its strategic and operational decisions on a timely and accurate basis, regardless of the type of decisions or where it is made.

While many financial systems are found to be "just adequate" for accounting purposes, they often fail to give requisite operating information to line managers or provide performance information to senior management on a timely basis. To be useful, strategic information must be compiled from the overabundance of operational data being stored; overnight batch reports are no longer sufficient. Managers need to operate with a bigger role in modeling the whole business operation. The ability to construct queries on the fly and to quickly ask follow-up questions that drill deeper into the data with each successive query is necessary to allow managers to better understand the business environment before making critical decisions. Changing market conditions and specific business situations, such as inventory levels and detailed analysis of customers' behavior, can point analysts down potential profitable paths that they could not have anticipated. For it to succeed in doing so, the systems should be developed to help managers make better strategic decisions.

New technology must be used to achieve better cost control. As businesses in the 1990's focus on downsizing and cost control as means to survive, there is a growing need for faster, more accurate, and more useful information that allows companies to perform better financial management. In more cases than not, this is easier said than done. Many companies, especially those that are large or highly decentralized, are finding it difficult to get at the information they need to effectively manage their business. These companies are often restrained by their inflexible legacy systems and an environment surrounded by non-standardization, creating difficulties in simple reorganization, much less using their financial information for better management in a rapidly changing world.

In regards to the lack of control in report generating, managers are faced with problems associated with bottlenecking. The report generating process often has difficulty integrating all the data required to make a comprehensive and informative assessment for managers to work with, often with high price tags, to suit. As companies become more widespread and powerful, the balance of data processing power has shifted away from central Information Systems staffs to individuals in functional departments. By tying together desktop computers, inexpensive Intranets enable businesses to integrate their information systems to a greater extent than was previously possible.

Clearly the need for integration is a key driver of the financial Intranet marketplace. Many organizations are planning to integrate their accounting systems into their networks over the next several years. Financial executives desire the ease of use and timeliness that this will afford. Information systems managers, faced with scarce resources, believe this will smooth out system development and management processes, saving time and money.

Financial Analysis and Management Accounting

While managing the transaction aspects of financial flows is important, there exists another facet, namely using financial information for control purposes. The area of financial management that is essential to support the operations and strategy of the company is called management accounting. Management accounting typically includes business planning, decision making, budgeting, and controlling, including *overhead cost* management, activity based costing, product cost controlling, and sales and profit analysis.

Gathering data for management accounting is quite challenging as few companies maintain a single, integrated set records for all their divisions and the departments within them. In practice, to consolidate their data, companies tie together data from many sources, including databases and spreadsheets. Bringing data together for periodic accounting, reporting, and budgeting has been difficult. The process adds to the time and cost required to perform consolidations at the end of a period, as well as to create and track budgets and forecasts. At the functional level, consolidation can provide the finance organization independence from the central IS organizations with a set of applications that are powerful but easy to use. This includes support for management accounting and cost accounting.

Once the data is gathered, financial analysis tools enable people with authorized access in the organization to find the data they need, drill down as necessary, and see the results in seconds, without waiting for MIS or even corporate accounting's involvement. This information is meant not only for executives, but also for a broader set of people who want to make better decisions on a daily basis.

Online Analytical Processing (OLAP)

Analytical tools, called OLAP, transforms the corporate data warehouse information into strategic information. For instance, users of financial data warehousing applications want better access and analysis of the data contained in the database archives. OLAP tools range from basic navigation and browsing to a multifaceted analysis of corporate data.

OLAP applications offer the advantage of spanning to a variety of organizational functions. Finance departments use OLAP for applications such as budgeting, activity-based costing, financial performance analysis, and financial modeling. Managers use these tools to perform ad hoc analysis of data in multiple dimensions, thereby giving them the insight and understanding they need for better decision making. OLAP lets managers probe and access corporate data in bits and pieces, rather than traditional means of query. This method gives the manager consistently fast access to a wide variety of views of data organized by criteria that match the real dimensions of the modern enterprise.

OLAP uses a multidimensional view of aggregate data to provide quick access to strategic information for further analysis. The key feature is the ability to transform data into so-called multidimensional form. These views are inherently representative of an actual business model. Managers typically look at financial data by scenario, organization, product line items, and time; and at sales data by product, geography, channel, and time. Database design should not prejudice which operations can be performed on a dimension or how rapidly those operations are performed. Managers must be able to analyze data across any dimension, at any level of aggregation, with equal functionality and ease. OLAP software should support these views of data in natural and responsive fashion, insulating users of the information from complex query syntax. After all, managers shouldn't have to understand complex computer languages to use OLAP.

Extranets

An *extranet* is an extended Intranet creating virtual private networks between companies, business partners, and clients. It allows intranets to interact. Security provides the appropriate level of access to users. The key point is that all three "nets"-- Internet, Intranet, and extranet--use the same technology. The only difference among them is who has access to what. The goal is to have access to what you need no matter where you are at any time of the day or night. No matter where you are when you log in, things should work the same way.

Companies can:
- Establish direct private network links between themselves, or create private secure Internet links between them, called *virtual private networks (VPNs)*.
- Use the unsecured Internet as the extranet link between its intranet and consumers and others, but rely on encryption of sensitive data and its own firewall systems to provide adequate security.

Business Value of Extranets

The business value of extranets is derived from several factors:
- The Web browser technology of extranets makes customer and supplier access of intranet resources a lot easier and faster than previous business methods
- Extranets enable a company to offer new kinds of interactive Web-enabled services to their business partners. Thus, extranets are another way that a business can build and strengthen strategic relationships with its customers and suppliers.
- Extranets enable and improve collaboration by a business with its customers and other business partners.
- Extranets facilitate an online, interactive product development, marketing, and customer-focused process that can bring better designed products to market faster.

Summary

The role of Intranets in supporting management is to meet their needs in acquiring comprehensive and timely business information. A company's accumulated data constitute a valuable resource, and in most organizations, those in charge are very aware of this fact, yet it is equally clear that the approach of simply collecting data has serious shortcomings. It neither succeeds in presenting data to corporate decision makers in a form they can understand and use, nor permits easy access to information.

Incompatible accounting and information systems are causing management tremendous problems. In the past, companies have attempted to support financial information systems by using mainframes that have been rigid in structure, expensive to maintain, and difficult to update when business requirements change. At the other end of the spectrum, firms generate business reports by assembling them manually by using spreadsheets and data from general ledgers and other operating systems. This approach would be incapable of handling large volumes of data primarily because it would require extensive data rekeying and manual consolidation. In addition, spreadsheets have limited capabilities for information sharing and lack the necessary control to ensure corporate consistency.

As business requirements have changed, there has been an increasing push toward the ability to analyze amounts of data in real-time. This enables management to look at different scenarios and make decisions in hours rather than in weeks. Inevitably, broad access to data and to the analytic tools that ease the analysis of the data will change the face of decision making. The speed and ease with which analysis can be completed and the inclusion of up-to-the-minute and on-the-fly accurate data are powerful competitive weapons.

Intranet technology can aid in the collection, aggregation, and consolidation of business information from fragmented computer systems and transactional databases in a number of ways, and in many cases Intranet developments will replace existing systems with more efficient alternatives.

Intranet applications can start as small "pilots" and scale upward over time, gradually providing or facilitating access to an increasing breadth of information, thus improving both employee productivity and satisfaction, and eventually bolstering the company's competitive position.

CHAPTER 5

Marketing and Advertising

The potential of the Internet and the World Wide Web (WWW) is most exciting. Online sales in year 2007 is expected to total over $100 billion, according to a report this week from ComScore Networks Inc. (www.comscore.com), a market research firm in Reston, Va. , accounting for 23% in computers, 13% in books, 10% in tickets, 9% in music/video, 8% in travel, 7% in toys, and 7% in consumer electronics.

The Internet allows retailers to reach both their customers and suppliers and provides another medium for retailers to expand internationally at a relatively low cost. Technology plays a vital role in business, helps improve efficiency, and allows businesses to provide higher value and greater convenience to their customers.

Many online retailers, such as the Amazon.com bookstore, PC makers such as Dell, and various flower and gift stores are thriving, proving that Internet retailing can work when properly done. The "best-of-breed" stores dominate each category; these specialized companies are able to out-innovate their competitors and retain customers.

While many business retailers, such as Amazon.com, are moving aggressively on to the Internet, many more are proceeding cautiously. Typically, the Internet is used as a means to advertise merchandise and a toll-free telephone number is provided for customer orders. Many retailers are reluctant to devote more resources to the Internet until they feel more confident of consumer interest.

Recent surveys indicate that Americans are concerned about giving credit card information online. The development of advanced cryptographic techniques is likely to alleviate this concern. For example, MasterCard and Visa are jointly developing Secure Electronic Transfer (SET) technology to make credit card transactions safer by encrypting the consumers' credit card numbers. Even the merchants will not even be able to see the credit card numbers. This will prevent unscrupulous merchants from selling some product over the Internet solely to collect credit card numbers. As technology improves and consumers become more comfortable with the Internet, it is likely that privacy/encryption issues will not be a serious barrier to Internet commerce.

Internet speed is holding back both consumers and retailers. The relatively slow speed means that consumers have to wait for images to download for viewing. However, with increased competition in the communications industry and broadband technology, consumers will benefit from faster and more affordable access to the Internet.

Selling merchandise over the Internet makes it possible to reach not only domestic consumers but also international consumers. Access to the Internet is generally more expensive outside the United States; the cost to connect to the Internet is sometimes two to three times the cost in the United States. The cost of connecting to the Internet will continue to decrease in the future worldwide. The rapid expansion of the Internet in the United States and internationally means that commercial web sites will become a profitable distribution channel for businesses.

Consumers are likely to benefit greatly from retailing on the Internet. Search engines are under development that will enable consumers to find merchandise on the Internet at the lowest price. This will lead to significant changes in the way business is conducted. There will be tremendous pressure on retailers to cut their margins. The competitive pressures are expected to result in a drop in retail prices of up to 30 percent over the next 10 to 15 years. Technology is being developed that will allow consumers to view 3-D images of the product. Instead of just reading a description and looking at a photograph, a consumer will be able to visually inspect the product at virtually any angle. It is clear that the Internet is going to be a major distribution channel for businesses in the near future. When shopping online, it is often easier for the customer to search and compare information on brands and prices.

The Internet can help a business do much more. The Internet is a great tool for conducting marketing research, including gathering primary and secondary data. Information is the key factor in electronic commerce.

Market Analysis

The Internet is a great source of primary and secondary marketing data. Businesses should not overlook the wealth of marketing information available on the Internet. Such information must be evaluated for credibility. Information on the Internet is not generally reviewed, evaluated, or censored by anyone other than the owner of the information. As such, the information may not necessarily be correct or reliable. On the other hand, information on the Internet can and is generally updated frequently.

Printed matter tends to become obsolete. The information on the Internet can be kept current and is accessible by anyone in the world, 24 hours a day. In the end, it is up to the market researcher to evaluate the quality of web related information.

Market research is an integral part of product development and design. Products should be tested at each design stage. This tends to be expensive and time consuming. Budgetary constraints sometimes limit a company's ability to properly conduct market research. Companies want to reduce the research time, as well as save on expenses.

One solution is interactive multimedia research which can have a company reach a greater number of markets and respondents. Using sound and video multimedia, researchers can test the design features of a new product. Multimedia research eliminates the need for developing actual prototypes or conducting tests using concept boards or story boards. Multimedia research also eliminates the need to make multiple copies of these items to use in several test markets.

Conventional market research techniques can lead to fatigue, boredom and strain on the respondents. To save time, respondents in a focus group may have to evaluate several concepts or designs in a single session. The stress caused by boredom or fatigue can affect objectivity and may lead to biased responses.

On the other hand, several markets can be tested simultaneously using multimedia research in significantly less time and money. Typically, a much greater number of concepts can be evaluated from a large number of respondents. A more diverse and representative sample can typically be obtained.

The primary disadvantage of interactive multimedia research is that physical substance is lacking. Respondents cannot touch, feel, manipulate, or use the product. For some products, this can lead to significant adverse effects. The disadvantages can be mitigated by providing some samples of the product along with multimedia sounds and video. The research process is unlikely to be affected. Reliability and validity are not affected, and the process is much shorter.

Secondary Data

Market researchers can collect and obtain information about consumers and competitors from the Net. Market research can help one determine the opportunities and pitfalls of a given strategy. Product mix and planning, pricing, promotion and distribution are all affected by market research data. While primary data may be collected, for example, from online surveys, it is often cost-effective to look at the secondary data online. Much of the secondary data is free and readily available. Demographic and cultural trends can be identified. Information is available about the economic, legal and political factors that affect marketing decisions. Information on competitors can easily be obtained online.

US Census Bureau

The US Census Bureau (www.census.gov) is an excellent source of demographic data. Like most government web sites, the information is free to users. While the official census takes place every ten years, more recent data is available from other surveys. A variety of data access tools are available to extract and display online information. Census Bureau information may be located by subject or topic. A keyword search may be performed on the online documents and files. Map searches through *DataMap* are available. *CenStats*, a web based subscription service, provides interactive search and display access to various databases. *CenStore* contains information about the various products sold by the Census Bureau and the U.S. Government Printing Office. An "economic clock" displays several current economic indicators including:

▶ U.S. International Trade in Goods and Services
▶ Advance Monthly Retail Sales
▶ Housing Starts
▶ Advance Report on Durable Goods Manufacturers' Shipments and Orders
▶ Manufacturers' Shipments, Inventories, and Orders
▶ Manufacturing and Trade Inventories and Sales
▶ Quarterly Financial Report for Manufacturing, Mining, and Trade Corporations

American Demographics Marketing Tools

The web site of American Demographics Marketing Tools (http://adage.com/americandemographics) contains a wealth of information. *American Demographics Magazine* provides consumer trends for business leaders. The web site allows users to view and search its databases. If users find the material useful, users are expected to subscribe to their print edition. Its *Marketing Tools* magazine provides information on marketing tactics and techniques. Its search engine allows one to search the publication archives and other information at this site by using keywords or phrases.

Business Marketing Association (BMA)

There is a difference in the needs of business marketers and consumer marketers. The Business Marketing Association (www.marketing.org) serves the needs of business-to-business marketers. It contains surveys, reports, newsletters, articles, etc. It has several hundred data files concerning marketing and communications. The site provides information about education, training, professional certification, membership benefits, and other resources.

U.S. Postal Service (USPS)

The U.S. Postal Service (www.usps.com) web site is an excellent source for postal information. ZIP+4 Code can be looked up. There is also a link to find out city and ZIP Code associations. It contains a frequently asked questions (FAQs) section. Information about preferred address abbreviations is available. It is possible to track express mail packages. Rate information is available.

Primary Data

When secondary data is not available, or when the marketing department decides to find its own information directly, primary data is collected. Primary data is collected and analyzed to solve a specific problem. It is generally cost-effective to use secondary data; primary data collection tends to be expensive and time consuming. However, primary data tends to be more relevant to the problem at hand.

Once the marketing problem is identified, a determination must be made of:
- the data needed to solve the problem
- who will provide the data
- how will the data be collected

Data collection is one activity that may successfully be done on the Internet. Two commonly used techniques are:
- sending questionnaires by email
- posting questionnaires on web sites

Collecting data on the Internet is generally much faster and economical than traditional techniques. It is often easier to elicit participation from online users. Net questionnaires are still somewhat novel and many people surfing the net may find it interesting to participate in the survey. However, participants may get upset if they are sent unwanted or "junk" email. The source of the email address is of special ethical concern. For example, it is unethical to obtain email addressed from newsgroups without permission.

Participants might be more truthful in their responses because they are interacting with a non-judgmental computer and not a human being. On the other hand, some participants may take advantage of their anonymity and answer the questions untruthfully. For example, they may lie about their age or sex.

Data captured electronically can easily be statistically analyzed and used. It is not prone to data entry errors by the researchers. Respondents are, however, more likely to make data entry mistakes. Respondents are less likely to make mistakes when writing than when typing. Researchers have some control over data entry mistakes by researchers' staff. Data can, for example, be checked by another individual for errors. This option is not available in electronically captured data. One way to overcome this problem is by building redundancy checks into questionnaires.

The Internet is diverse. A large number of users from all over the world can participate in the marketing study. This means the researcher may have little control over who participates in the study and the resulting sample size. While caution must be exercised when collecting primary data on the Internet, exciting new possibilities are available.

Developing Web Sites

Interactive Web Sites

Successful web sites provide valuable information beyond what is available in print or by what is available from competing businesses. The content should be relevant, reliable, and accurate. It should be possible for a customer to quickly and easily locate the needed information. It should be easy to navigate the web site. The information of the web site should download quickly. Extensive graphics and multimedia capabilities can considerably slow the downloading process and may frustrate customers. This involves, in part, having a good understanding of the type of equipment and communication lines used by your customers.

Creating and maintaining an interactive web site is typically technologically complex and requires much greater resources. Frequently, companies forego interactive pages and place ads with only product and price information. It is hoped that web surfers will automatically be motivated to buy their product. It is dangerous to make this assumption. Users on the net can choose between thousands and thousands of sites. Every company needs to capture roaming surfers. Success on the net requires developing customers and serving them well. One successful technique is to offer web visitors special deals. It is beneficial to fully integrate net operations with other types of marketing activities. The web site must be designed so that it is appropriate for the target audience.

From a technical perspective it is undesirable to use too much technology. The web site should not be testing the latest gizmos. Such things can often detract from building suitable sites. Programming is generally required to develop high quality interactive web sites. PERL (Practical Extraction and Report Language) is used extensively in practice. It is available for free and enough programmers know PERL to provide on-going support. When designing web pages, dimensions of the graphics should always be included in the HTML code for faster displays. It is easy to add free features, such as Real Audio and Real Video (www.real.com) to the web site.

Several search engines are available either for free or for at a nominal cost. Some search engines, however, tend to be expensive and can cost several thousand dollars. With limits on download speeds, it is imprudent to have too much in graphics or animation at a web site. However, as download speeds increase in the future, the

Web graphics are likely to change from two-dimensional to three-dimensional (3-D). 3-D imaging technology will greatly assist consumers in making purchases over the Internet. Instead of just reading a description and looking at a photograph, a consumer will be able to visually inspect the product at virtually any angle. Marketers should be following closely new developments in 3-D technology.

3-D graphics and virtual reality modeling language (VRML) applications are increasingly popular. These technologies require faster processors and modems, increased bandwidth capacities, graphics accelerators, and better authoring tools. Web browsers will have to support 3-D technology.

Web designers and marketers are offering custom web pages for the visitor. They can create highly personalized Web pages and increase the likelihood of future visits. For example, the computer could monitor a visitor's interest in the various items at the web site and process that information to personalize the web page for each visitor. Alternatively, the visitor could answer a few questions about specific interests and receive a customized web page.

Product development lead time is expected to be reduced with 3-D modeling. Multimedia techniques such as interactive applications with 3-D modeling, animation, video, and sound are offering companies of all types with new ways to market their products. Well designed multimedia tools make it easy to market and sell products or services; they offer speed, accuracy and easy updates. Multimedia presentations are generally more refined, and may even eliminate the need for salespeople.

Interactive multimedia brochures are becoming increasing popular; presently, it is an effective supplement to printed matter. The cost of developing interactive web sites is higher than the cost of producing a typical printed color brochure. However, companies integrating interactive multimedia technology into their marketing plans are seeing positive results.

Companies frequently release images of the product when making new product announcements. Sometimes, the design process is not even complete when these announcements are made. Companies benefit from customer feedback and gain insight into whether the product should be developed further. Developing actual prototypes is either too expensive or simply unfeasible. 3-D modeling is an effective way to show how the product works and to create an illusion that the product actually exists.

The web site should have search capabilities. The web site should be easy to navigate. Visitors should be able to find information quickly and easily. The material should be kept current and updated frequently. Let the users know the last time the material was updated.

A tremendous amount of work is required to set up and maintain the web site. Do not underestimate the number of visitors. Both the underlying technology as well as personal effort should be carefully considered. Basic rules should be established at an initial stage. A decision must be made about the degree of control that will be exercised by your firm. For example, will the chat rooms be extensively controlled and moderated, or will users be able to say and post anything? From a legal perspective, it is prudent to include a statement with all online messages stating that the views expressed are those of the users and not the company or its management and the company is not responsible for the content.

If you wish to moderate discussions, be prepared to read all posted messages. Alternatively, consider enlisting the help of some volunteers to act as moderators; you can reward the moderators by giving them special discounts or other benefits. Moderators should be provided with editorial rules and policies. They should be able to change discussion topics, as necessary. At the same time, do not over-moderate. Let the users talk about what they want, otherwise they are likely to lose interest.

When setting up the web site, a system should be installed to measure if the goals are being accomplished. For example, your goal may to bring in a certain number of new members. Progress towards goals should be appropriately documented. For instance:

- Are more people joining your community than leaving your community? What is the net gain per week or per month?
- Where are the new members coming from?
- Are existing members referring new members?
- Are existing members satisfied?
- What are the buying habits of members?

Basic precautions should be taken when building your company's web site. Don't expect your visitors to have the latest and best equipment. Keep in mind that many users will not update to the latest version of the browser or other software. Try to make the web page easy to view on different size monitors.

Building Customer Loyalty

Building a virtual online community is an excellent way to attract visitors to your web site. Individuals with different motivations are going to be attracted to such a site. Some users are just browsers. They may be curious or just looking for certain information. Such individuals are unlikely to participate extensively in the online community. Other users may have a problem and want help from other individuals who have previously encountered the same problem. Still others may be interested primarily in offering their expertise. Such communities work because users enjoy being a part of the community and enjoy discussions of its main topic.

The aim should be to build an online community that is self-sufficient. No formal supervision should be needed. Members should monitor and police themselves. Allowing users to download files makes the site significantly more attractive. Providing answers to Frequently Asked Questions (FAQs) is extremely helpful. An automatic response system can answer or email responses to commonly asked questions to users. Many communities provide links to other similar sites.

Some online communities offer special events. Setting up specific times for special discussions is an excellent way to encourage users to visit your site. Special events may host a well known expert on the topic. Top management should also participate on a periodic basis. Special discounts should be offered to regular visitors to your site.

The increased use of electronic commerce is likely to lead to lower prices. Customers will be more easily able to compare prices and play one vendor off another. Vendor's delivery costs are likely to be reduced and customers will demand concessions. Many transaction costs will be reduced with automated negotiations. While customers want a low price, that is not the only factor that affects their decisions. With reduced profit margins, for companies to survive, they must have a strategy for growth and provide value-added-services.

One option is to create a web site that is not purely self-serving. The web site should be a source of information to the consumer and not just another place for a company's "hype." The site should allow customers or potential customers to interact with each other. Saturn has had considerable success allowing its car buying customers access to each other. Customers should be allowed to discuss the product's price, quality, etc. without censorship from the sponsor of the web site. For example, Amazon. com allows customers to post online book reviews.

Online customers want instant responses. Email should be responded to quickly. On time delivery of products is another key factor in gaining customer loyalty.

It is important to put the customers' interest first. Customers are likely to develop loyalty to a company's brand or product if the company makes them feel important. Loyalty generates repeat purchases. This is especially important because the cost of retaining customers is significantly lower than the cost of acquiring new ones. Repeat customers are also likely to spend more on purchases than new customers. Incentives and electronic coupons are often successful in encouraging individuals to visit a specific web site. Online customers are generally more educated consumers and demand a better value for their money.

Many prospective customers are not immediately ready to buy. The aim should be to encourage visitors to take action and request information such as a brochure, catalog, or price quotation. It should be easy for visitors to send you email. A "hot link" to your email address should appear on each web page. Email addresses from these individuals should be saved to create a mailing list. New product announcements and news releases should be sent to these individuals. Always give individuals the option to remove their name from the mailing list.

Sending unsolicited email is not generally a good way to increase web traffic. Mass unsolicited commercial email is known as "spam." Unsolicited or "junk" email is, at a minimum, a source or nuisance to web users. Junk email may also be considered as an invasion of privacy by some. Sending junk mail costs money with no revenue benefits. The Internet transcends national boundaries. It is necessary for business to design the web site to suit local needs. A single web site is unlikely to serve the needs of the entire world. Businesses must be prepared to comply with the different rules and regulations of other countries. A different strategy will generally be needed for penetrating markets in each new country.

The rate of growth of US web users is expected to decrease, while the rate of growth of users in the rest of the world is expected to increase. The overseas growth opportunities are simply tremendous. Most of the growth in the Internet is expected to come from business-to-business transactions.

Advertising Web Site

Internet advertising is a relatively new field. While most firms spend a significant amount on advertising, their budget for Internet advertising is relatively small. It is clear that the Internet's share in total advertising expenditures will grow. Internet offers new opportunities to marketers. It is easier to target customers on the Internet. Hence, advertising on the Internet is more effective and efficient. It is possible to provide customers with detailed product information and specifications. Internet advertising is an active, not passive, activity. Advertising is used to accomplish several objectives:

- To inform consumers
- To increase demand
- To increase or decrease demand elasticity
- To discourage entry by potential competitors
- To differentiate the firm from existing competitors

Many aspects of Internet advertising are different from broadcasting and mass media advertising. There are two models of advertising: the "push" model, and the "pull" model. In the push model, the seller selects its target audience and decides on the content of the advertisement. In the pull model, buyers have greater input. Both the push and pull models are used extensively on the Internet.

Traditional types of marketing and selling techniques are not as successful on the Internet. Traditionally, the marketing strategy was to broadcast to a vast number of prospective customers. Media such as radio, television, billboards, newspapers, etc. are used to deliver short, high impact messages. The media space is limited and sells at a premium price. The advertiser can fit only a little information in the limited space. Hence, the advertiser's aim to create and project an intangible image of quality.

Unwanted broadcast type advertising is likely to receive a negative reaction from online users. Some network service providers have specific rules against unwanted advertising. People on the Internet want interactivity. In contrast, passive (one way advertising) is the norm with traditional broadcast advertising. For companies to succeed, they should provide a high level of interactivity. Information content should be relevant and detailed.

Storage capacity on the Internet is virtually unlimited and very inexpensive; you don't have to pay a premium for limited advertising space. Vast amount of information can be shared with interested customers. The Internet's navigation tools help customers find exactly the information they need. The interactive nature of the Internet also means that prospective customers can ask questions and communicate directly with the information provider.

Banner Ads

Banner ads are one popular form of online advertising. Banner ads are graphic images in Web pages that are often animated and can include small pieces of software code to allow further interaction. Most importantly, they are "clickable," and take a viewer to another Web location when chosen.

Banner ads typically run at the top and bottom of the page, but they can be incorporated anywhere. The CASIE organization has developed a small number of standard sizes and formats. Like the Web itself, banner ads are a mixture of approaches, with elements of traditional print advertising and more targeted direct advertising. Banner ads include direct marketing capabilities. Each banner carries with it a unique identifier. This allows the Web site to track the effectiveness of the ad in generating traffic. Measurability permits ad banner pricing based on results and behavior. Click-through pricing ignores impressions and charges the advertiser based on the number of viewers that select the ad and follow it to the linking Web site.

Admittedly, the performance of banner ads to date has been less than stellar. One company, San Francisco-based Organic, has approached the problem of ineffective online advertising with a product called "expand-o." This new ad vehicle allows an advertiser to include some of its Web site's content in an expandable banner ad. At the click of a mouse, the advertisement expands to as much as five or six times its original size. For instance, an expand-o for Fort Washington, PA-based CDNow provides consumers with a sample of dynamically updated content housed on the music retailer's site. When the consumer clicks an arrow on the ad, it expands to show the top 10 songs in CDNow's top 100 Billboard Chart.

Playing the Search-Engine Game

More and more companies doing business online find that the best way to reach prospective customers is through their Web searches. After all, most customers looking to make a purchase online start with a keyword search. Results like that are fueling rapid growth in the industry. Spending on paid listings, paid inclusion, and search engine optimization—the three forms of search-related marketing—globally is expected to grow to about $7 billion a year by 2007 from $2 billion in 2004.

Paid listings—The hottest category in search marketing is paid listings—short text advertisements, with links to the advertiser's site, that appear on the pages that display the results of an Internet search. Marketers refer to these ads as pay for placement, pay for performance, pay per click or cost per click—terms that reflect how the system works for advertisers.

Paid inclusion—Paid listings can be pricey, particularly for companies whose product lines are so complex ad fluid that they would have to buy listings for a multitude of keywords and continually buy new ones to cover their inventory. For these companies especially, an alternative, paid inclusion, can be an effective way to increase visibility on the Web. In paid inclusion, a company pays a search engine for the right to submit the entire content of its Web site, or selected pages, directly to the search engine's database.

Search-engine optimization—This term is defined as the act of altering a company's Web site so that it may rank well for particular terms' used in Web searches. The idea is to get the company's site to the top of the results of a Web search, or at least on the first page of the results. One relatively easy change to make is to use simple terms or words that everyone would understand to describe your products—and therefore be more likely to use in a search—instead of industry jargon.

Web Storefronts

Creating and maintaining a web site or a web storefront can involve considerable expenditure. However, most businesses simply can't ignore this medium. The web site typically contains information about the company and its products. Consumers generally have more confidence in sales advice provided through a web site than in sales advice given by humans; there is generally a distrust of salespersons. Computerized sales information is uniform and has greater credibility. People perceive that computers have no incentive to lie.

Most companies now have at least a basic web site. Some points to consider are:

- Who are your customers likely to be?
- What profile and characteristics do customers possess?
- Where are desirable types of customers likely to be on the Internet?
- What type of mailing lists or new groups do targeted customers use? Mailing lists and news groups tend to be highly specialized. They tend to concentrate on very specific topics.
- What will turn customers "on" or "off?"

To achieve the maximum return on investment from the Internet, marketing managers must find ways of integrating online marketing with their general marketing program. The Internet offers significant benefits to customers. For example, it makes it easier and faster for customers to find and purchase items. Customers can check for product availability and get specifications and pricing information twenty-four hours a day. Implementing such features frequently leads to higher sales and cost savings in providing customer service.

Advertising the company's web site is critical. Customers must know about the web site before they can use it. All printed matter, as well as any other media, should encourage users to visit the web site. All ads, brochures, business cards, letterheads, and any other material should have your web site address on it. The web site address should receive the same prominence as an organization's address or phone number.

Search engines, such as Yahoo!, Excite, and Lycos are an excellent source of web visitors. The web site should be registered on as many search engines as possible; at the very least, it should be registered on all major search engines. It is prudent to re-register after a few months to enhance the chances of your web site appearing in a person's search. The home page should contain invisible key words or "metatags." If any key word on your home page matches a customer's search request, your web site will be listed.

Reciprocal linking arrangements are a great way to make your site known. Related sites should be requested to include links to your site. An additional advantage of this approach is that as some search engines capture link data from web sites, your company's web site is more likely to be found by visitors.

Another approach to consider is Web directories advertising. Such listings generally cost a few hundred dollars per year.

A company should not abandon its successful marketing practices just because it is now marketing on the Internet. Marketing strategies that work in basic print are likely to work on the web as well. For example, if a company offers certain promotions to its print customers and the promotions have been beneficial, offering the same promotions on the Internet should be beneficial.

However, the benefits of the electronic and interactive nature of the Internet should not be ignored. The Internet is not simply a passive print media. It is much easier for marketers to learn the browsing and purchasing habits of Internet customers. Such data can be captured automatically. Such data can also be provided by the customers; customers may be asked to fill an interactive questionnaire and provide their name, address, telephone number, and other information if they want to receive a free catalog of the company's products.

The Internet presents the marketers with new and unique opportunities and only companies that successfully exploit these opportunities will succeed in the competitive world of electronic commerce. It is essential to offer customers the ability to purchase products online. Online customers want instant information. At a minimum, they want to know the description and features of a product, its price, current inventory status, how long it will take for them to get it, and the company's return policy.

Email is now a key channel of communication between companies and their customers. Resources should be budgeted to develop email content and to deliver it to a great number of individuals. There are several specialized companies that specialize in delivering customized email messages to a vast number of individuals. Sending unsolicited email on the Internet often does not pay off. Email should generally be sent only to those individuals that have requested information.

To get people to read your email, you must build a relationship with them. Address the individuals personally and maintain a personal contact. Sending unsolicited bulk email is generally not illegal. Some jurisdictions require that the return address on the email be real. Many Internet users, however, consider it a nuisance. Still, it is popular because it's considerably cheaper than traditional bulk postage mailing. Sending unsolicited email can cause many problems. The Internet culture has a strong bias against any type of a sales pitch. Recipients of unsolicited email will often complain to your Internet Service Provider (ISP) and many ISP will terminate accounts of companies that send junk mail.

It is possible to send commercial email to recipients that have given permission to receiving commercial email. Many companies specialize in such type of direct email marketing. While this targeted direct email marketing is more expensive than unsolicited junk email, it is often far more effective.

An extensive list of opt-in email lists is available from The Directory Email List Source (www.copywriter.com/lists). Other businesses that specialize in providing "opt-in" mailing lists include: www.bulletmail.com and www.postmasterdirect.com.

Opt-in mail lists work because businesses and consumers are given incentives to receive commercial email messages. Sometimes different types of web promotions such as contests and sweepstakes are used to encourage individuals to visit clients' web sites. Such promotional campaigns often cost significantly less than long-term banner advertisements. Consumers are willing to volunteer their time and attention in return for some type of reward. People are willing to disclose information about themselves and you can tell them about your product.

Banner ads are very common and useful on the web. The purpose of banner ads is to catch the Internet user's attention. Banner ads should have a colorful background. They should contrast with the background web page. It is easier to read dark text off light background. Use animation to draw attention. However, don't become obtrusive and keep the animation simple. Don't use deceptive techniques since it may frustrate or anger the consumer.

A successful Internet marketing technique is to have a sign-up form on your web site to allow visitors to register for an e-mail newsletter. An organization or individual that sends spam is demonstrating that they do not care about their reputations; it is unwise to do business with such a party.

Many individuals hesitate to remove themselves from a spam list; responding to a spammers email may act as a signal to confirm that the recipient is reading the e-mail and may therefore receive even more junk mail. It is also unfair to have the recipient spend time trying to remove themselves from the mailing list.

The online bookseller Amazon.com offers its visitors a valuable service. Visitors may register to receive email whenever new books on specified topics become available. Some travel club web sites will email members when new discounts on airlines or travel packages become available. Users may sign up to receive a newsletter or reminder; users give permission to be contacted again via email.

Instructions should be included at the beginning and end of all email messages letting recipients know how they can remove their name permanently from future mailings. You may also ask members to forward your email message to people they know who share similar interests.

Signature files should be used whenever you send email. The signature file contains information such as your Uniform Resource Locator (URL) and email address. Individuals may use it to contact you. It is like handing out your electronic business card and it is unobtrusive as long as you do not include too much information in it.

Electronic Assurance Services

To give consumers greater confidence in transacting online, the American Institute of Certified Public Accountants (AICPA) and the Canadian Institute of Chartered Accountants (CICA) have jointly developed the "WebTrust" program. It is a type of electronic seal which provides certain assurances. A Certified Public Accountant (CPA), who is a member of the AICPA or a Chartered Accountant (CA), who is a member of the CICA, is able to perform a WebTrust examination. The WebTrust seal on a web site indicates that a CPA (or CA in Canada) has evaluated a particular web site's business practices and controls and the site meets all of the WebTrust criteria. After issuing the initial WebTrust seal, the CPA must perform an update at least quarterly to make sure that all guidelines for authenticity, security, and privacy have been followed by the web site.

Selling Online

Providing the ability to order online enhances the likelihood of a sale. It is much easier for a customer to click the "purchase" button on a web site than to call the company and give his or her name and product number and other information. However, in most instances, customers should not be forced to order only through the Internet.

79

Many customers don't yet feel comfortable about giving their credit card numbers over the Internet. Giving such customers a choice, such as ordering through the telephone or fax, would help increase the company's sales.

Online ordering gives a company a marketing edge. It is easy to take advantage of the interactive nature of the Internet and track a visitor's browsing habits. If your tracking program notices that an individual has repeatedly visited your web site without placing an order, a special offer could be made to that individual to encourage him to place an order.

Cross-selling is another advantage of online ordering. Assume a customer is ordering a backpacking tent from a sporting goods web site. This provides you with a wealth of information and creates a great cross-selling opportunity. For example, you can remind the customer to purchase a sealant to water-proof the tent, or a tarpaulin to protect the tent floor. Such customers might also be interested in purchasing hiking shoes, backpacks, sleeping bags, trail maps, insect repellents, and other similar items.

For instance, a sporting goods web site could offer customers a chance to browse through your "hiking checklist" to ensure they haven't forgotten something important, such as a first aid kit, for their hiking trip. However, the checklist should not be self-serving. The checklist should be of value to consumers. It should not simply be a list of items you wish to sell to customers.

The checklist should contain items that are needed in hiking, and not only the items your company sells. For example, while your company may not sell portable water purification systems, these items should be included in the checklist. Furthermore, you may want to provide links to other web sites that sell water purification systems. An added advantage of this may be that the linked site may include a reciprocal link back to your company's web site.

Make it easy for the customer to make an informed purchase decision. Customers can be encouraged to upgrade their product choices. Many individuals may be willing to spend more for a better quality product if they are educated on its benefits. Quantity discounts may be offered to encourage further sale.

Printed brochures and catalogs are generally expensive, are limited in space, and typically become outdated quickly. On the other hand, space on the Internet is inexpensive, virtually unlimited, and the information on it can be updated quickly. For example, if you see that a product's sales are below expectation, a special discount can instantly be offered to encourage sales.

Customers should be allowed to save their purchase orders. It should be easy for them to add or delete items as they browse through the web site. If they don't wish to order or pay for the products immediately, they should be given the option to save their purchase list till a later time. Make it easy for customers to order the same products again, or to modify their previous orders. The ordering process should be kept clear and simple. If certain customers are offered special prices, such adjustments should occur automatically.

It is possible to purchase keywords on search engines such as Yahoo! or Alta Vista. Each time a user types a search phrase that matches those keywords, your company's advertising banner will appear along with the search results. This can help increase visits to your web site significantly.

Customer Service

Email should be responded to with vigilance. Online customers demand immediate feedback and not responding to customers' email in a timely manner is a sure way to lose customers. If staff requirements make it impossible to respond in a timely manner (generally within 24 hours), at least an automated response should be immediately sent to the customers acknowledging receipt of their message. Automated systems are useful for answering frequently asked questions. Automated systems should be monitored because they can sometimes fail due to bugs or other problems. Customers want humans to respond to their messages and may be unhappy with an automated response.

When responding to a question, make sure you understand the question and your reply clearly addresses the specific problem. Do not respond in generalities, be precise and specific. After a reasonable interval, send a follow-up email to ensure that the customer is satisfied and his concerns have been addressed. Be polite in responding to customers' messages. Even if a customer is rude, do not confront the customer. Be empathetic and try to understand their problems.

Legal Issues in Advertising and Marketing

Caution should be exercised when setting up links to other web sites from your web site. Most webmasters want to publicize their site. Webmasters request links from directories and related sites and submit their URLs to search engines. However, recent litigation suggests that such links may not always be welcomed. For example, Microsoft Corp. was sued by Ticketmaster Corp. for what has become known as "deep linking." A click at Microsoft's site took users to a page deep within Ticketmaster's site. Such linking deprived Ticketmaster out of advertising dollars from banner ads that were bypassed. In addition, Microsoft's advertising revenue increased through the use of Ticketmaster's trademarks. See http://legal.web.aol.com/decisions/dlip/tickcomp.html.

In another case, *The Washington Post* sued Total News for linking to its web site. Total News had created a Web site that linked to 1,200 news sites. A click on Total News' site caused The Washington Post's news page to be brought up in a frame within the Total News' site. Only the Total News URL was displayed in the browser. The Washington

Post argued that that Total News had unfairly used its property. This case was settled out of court when Total News agreed to cease its framing practices.

It is prudent to include disclaimers that indicate the origin of the source of linked materials. You should also include a message stating that you will remove any link if requested by the owner of the linked web site. To prevent others from deep linking, several options are available. For example, you can use dynamic URLs which permit access to internal pages only from pages within the site.

Tracking Web Traffic

Tracking web traffic is an integral part of marketing research. You need to know how many individuals visited your site and how many people are viewing each of the pages. Web servers can track information from each request. Typically, you can get information about:

- the name of the host
- the visitor's login name, if authentication is mandatory
- the date and time of the "hit"
- the type of request
- who referred the user
- the visitor's "IP" address
- the number of bytes transferred
- "cookies" (electronic data) sent by the visitor
- "cookies" (electronic data) sent by the Web server
- the path of the file served

There is a distinction between a "hit" and a "pageview." A hit is recorded when any file (graphic, sound, etc.) is requested from the server. For instance, if a request is made for a page that contains five graphics the access log will count five hits. In contrast, the pageview measure indicates when a page as a whole is viewed. It is relatively easy to determine the number of hits to a site using a "hit counter." For a more accurate analysis, information in the web server logs should be analyzed. Analyzing logs will give you information about the number of failed hits as well as their status code.

Generally, pageview information is more useful. However, it is a little more difficult to get pageview information. You must differentiate between hits that are or are not pageviews. Common ways of doing this are by looking at the type of file, such as HTML or graphic, or sound. You might also be able to differentiate based upon the name of the file requested from the server. Looking at the web server's response code is yet another option. You may also want to differentiate between internally versus externally generated pageviews. You want to know the pageviews not only for your home page, but other pages as well. It is possible that users may have bypassed your home page and linked directly to one of your other pages.

It is useful to know where visitors are coming from. Are they coming from an advertisement banner? Are they coming from a link at another web site? Pageviews by referrer can help you determine if the banner advertisement is worthwhile. It will also give you some insight into the interests of your visitors by looking at the referring site. The referrer log can be useful in determining what links are proving most useful. You can determine the host of visitors. For example, how many people are coming from America Online or CompuServe or other service provider?

Pageview analysis can be done by time of day. This will tell you when individuals are accessing your site. It will also give you some insight into whether your site is being accessed during work hours or after work hours. Most home users dial up with slower speed modems. If most visits are after working hours, use fewer graphics for faster downloads. It is possible to determine the hardware platform (PC versus Mac) operating system being used by the visitor. It is also possible to determine the type of browser and its version. The Agent log records information about the browser, file transfer protocol (FTP) client, or search engine robot that accessed the web page. If different types of browsers with different capabilities or different versions are being used by a substantial number of visitors, it might make sense to offer pages in dual versions.

It is generally more difficult to determine the number of visitors than it is to determine the number of pageviews. You may not know if the same person is repeatedly viewing your pages or different individuals are accessing your pages. The following information may be used to track visitors:

- ▶ "IP" address
- ▶ user names (if registration is required)
- ▶ "cookies" (electronic data) -- bits of information stored on a client computer.

A visitor's IP address is perhaps the easiest way of counting visitors. By counting the number of unique IP addresses, you can get an approximation of the number of visitors. However, this method tends to be inaccurate or unreliable. One reason for inaccurate results is that most individuals get a different IP address each time they connect. Many ISPs assign addresses dynamically in order to use the IP addresses more efficiently. When the first visitor disconnects, the same IP address is available to another customer. A unique IP address does not necessarily mean that the same visitor came to your site twice. This method may give a reasonable approximation if the results are tabulated over a relatively short period of time. Over an extended period, accuracy decreases significantly.

Some sites require visitors to register and log in using their user name. This makes tracking visitors much easier. There is always the possibility that two or more individuals, such as spouses, will share the same user id and password. Moreover, unless you can justify why logging and authentication is necessary, many people will not visit your web site. Some sites reward people for the extra effort involved in logging in by providing special access to registered users.

"Cookies" can help you determine the number of visitors. It is possible to define a cookie that will have a unique value for each visitor. Some people, however, may turn off cookies in their web browser. They may also delete cookies at some time. Hence, even this may not be a reliable measure of visitors.

It is prudent to use a combination of IP addresses, user names, and cookies to determine web traffic. The most accurate way to gather visitor data is through a user name and password. Then you can track members' travels through your site with cookies or server objects. Keep in mind, that many users don't like the authentication process. In fact, such authentication could end up reducing web traffic.

The web server log should be analyzed on a periodic basis. The log contains vital information. It can help you understand your visitors. For most businesses, a weekly analysis of the logs should be sufficient. The analysis can be performed easily using a log file analysis program. You should find out how visitors found your site. This can help you increase traffic to your site. For example:

- What key words did visitors use on the search engine to locate your site?
- What search engines appear most frequently in the log files?
- Are some search engines missing from the log file?
- Did most visitors enter through your home page?
- From what pages do most of the visitors exit?
- What pages are popular or unpopular?
- What path through the web site is taken by most users?
- Do the popular pages have something in common?
- What is wrong with the unpopular pages and how may they be improved?
- Are other sites linking to pages with greater traffic?
- What pages on your site generate the most sales leads?
- Is there a navigation problem? If so, how may it be corrected?

Traffic log analysis will help you improve your site. For example, you could include something on pages from which most visitors exit to keep the visitors' interest and guide them to other pages on your site. You should develop a profile of your visitors. This will help you determine if you are attracting your target audience.

- Why did they visit?
- Where did they come from?
- Individuals from what kind of organizations are visiting your site?
- What country are they coming from?
- What pages did they view?
- Did they request anything via email?
- Did they download anything?

Web servers store different kinds of information in separate files, generally in ASCII format. Web-site analysis software can transform raw data into useful information, including providing charts, tables, graphs and reports. Most software packages analyze web server log files. All errors encountered during the visit are logged, including time-outs, lost connections, 404 (Not Found), and other types of failures. Scanning error reports can help you determine if you have missing files and your visitors have been having trouble accessing pages.

All log file analyzers share certain basic features. They can analyze files from several types of servers. However, such software packages differ in their ability to analyze files. Some programs require that you transfer the log files to the vendor for analysis. This is especially helpful if the log files are very large. The internal computer does not have to process the data. There is also the benefit of added credibility since the results are analyzed by a third-party. However, if you want to keep the information confidential, log file analysis software packages are available for in-house use. The following criteria will help you determine if the software package is suitable:

- Will the package produce the types of reports, charts, tables, and graphs that you need?
- Can the software package process log files typically generated by your server? (Many packages cannot handle very large log files.)
- Is the package easy to learn and use?
- Is the software available for your platform? Is it available for multiple platforms? Basic packages run on your web server and automatically generate reports. More advanced programs offer sophisticated analysis, but are typically run on a separate system.
- Does the software have to be run locally? Or, can it access the log files at other sites?
- Does the package offer database capabilities?
- Can the software import/export in different file formats?
- Does the package offer data drill-down capabilities? How many layers of data can you view and analyze?
- Does the package allow you to analyze data based on different units of time, such as hourly, daily, weekly, monthly, quarterly, annually?
- Can the log file analyzer automatically resolve numeric IP addresses and provide information about those visiting your site?
- How large a site can the software handle? Will you outgrow it quickly?
- How many sites can the software handle? Can it track several sites at once? If you have several web sites, can the software do a meta-analysis of all your sites?
- Does it offer real-time report access? For example, can you analyze data involving the last 10 minutes of your web site activity?

▶ Does the software package offer data integration and synthesis capabilities? Can it integrate sales and other business information, whether or not it is web based?

▶ How much does the software package cost? Will a shareware or freeware package do? Or, do you need a comprehensive package capable of advanced analysis?

The number of pageviews can sometimes be misleading. People may be visiting your site, but not sticking around long enough to read your message. This may happen if your graphics take too long to download.

Before reports, tables and charts can be generated, the log analyzer packages typically need to process log-file data. This is a time consuming process. Larger files can take a considerable amount of time for conversion. All the log analysis packages include some predefined reports and offer the ability to build custom reports using data filters. Traffic analysis software packages have their limitations. For instance, they do not provide any information about server reliability or integrity. Furthermore, if you need independently audited statistics of web traffic, you must enlist the services of external firms that specialize in providing audited data. Typically, reports produced by web traffic analysis packages include:

▶ the number of times specific pages were requested over a given period of time

▶ most frequently downloaded pages

▶ least frequently downloaded pages

▶ trends for visitor activity at specific times of the day or days of the week

▶ the most common entry points into your site

▶ the most common exit points from your site

▶ average time per visit (usually in seconds)

Organizing your web site

Each web *site* contains one or more web *presentations*. If the site contains only one presentation, the term web site and presentation are often used interchangeably. Each web presentation consists of one or more web *pages*. The *home* page is the first page of your web presentation. The key to organizing a web site is to answer a few basic questions:

▶ What is the purpose of your web site?

▶ What type of information do you want visitors to see?

▶ Why are people visiting your site?

▶ Are visitors looking for specific information?

▶ Are the visitors going to read each page in detail, or are they just going to scan it?

Your web site should include information about your company. Typical items to include in the company profile are as follows:

- what does the company do or sell, its various products and their prices
- new product announcements
- company's address, phone number and other location related information
- customer service and support information
- company policies
- job openings at the company
- company's financial information, including its stock-market symbol, the exchange it trades on, and current and historical share prices
- visitor guest-book to learn the profile of prospective customers
- online survey to get feedback from visitors on everything from your company's products to your web site
- links to other related sites

It should always be possible for the user to determine exactly where they are in your web site.

There are several ways to organize web presentations.

- A *linear* structure is very simple. It is just like a printed document. Its inflexible and rigid structure is ideal for situations where you do not want web visitors to skip around; that is, you want them to read the information in a strict order. The entire web presentation should not be in a linear structure. It should be used only in limited situations where such rigidity is warranted.
- In a *hierarchical* or *tree* structure, you start with a main menu. Visitors select a topic from the main menu and then from a sub-menu, and so forth. It is easy for visitors to navigate and know their exact position. Each hierarchical level should have a consistent interface. Too many levels should be avoided. Users can easily get frustrated if they have to search through several pages to find information.
- A combination of *linear and hierarchical* structures is popular. It is commonly used when multiple linear documents are put online. The FAQ (frequently asked questions) section of web sites typically follows this structure. The visitor is allowed to move vertically (hierarchical) as well as horizontally (linear). This can sometimes be confusing and individuals may have trouble navigating. Links should be provided on each page to move forward and backward, as well as the option to return to the beginning.
- A *web* structure is free-flowing. It has little or no structure. It is useful when the content is not directly related. It encourages users to browse. Its structure is almost like a maze and it is easy for users to get lost in the web

structure. Always provide a way for users to get back to the home page. A map of the overall structure is extremely helpful. The map does not necessarily have to be a visual map. It should convey enough information to keep the user oriented.

Visitors are not going to have the patience to remain at your site if the material is not properly organized. Most users will scan or browse and will not read everything. You must catch a prospective customer's eye quickly. The following points should be considered:

- Headings should be used to summarize topics.
- Menu links should be provided to enhance navigation. Always have a link to the home page.
- Lists should be used to summarize related items.
- Important information should be highlighted or emphasized, but don't overemphasize. It tends to make things unreadable.
- Paragraphs should be kept short. The most important information should appear in the first sentence.
- Each web page should be complete by itself. The user should be able to jump into your web and still have a sense of orientation.
- Each link should serve a purpose. Ensure that it is relevant to the content.
- Use graphic images, but don't overdo it. Keep the images small. Consider download times when using graphics or animation.
- Don't split topics across pages. Keep related items together. If the topic is too large for a single page, break it into self-contained sub-topics. Don't create too many or too few pages.
- Include information about the Webmaster and his or her email address.
- Don't forget to include copyright or trademark or service mark information.
- Include the URL of each page at the bottom. This is especially helpful if users print your pages. At a later time, they will be able identify where they got the information.

Storefront and Shopping Cart Software

A "shopping cart" program is essential for any business that wants to sell multiple products over the Internet. The software runs on the Internet Service Provider's computer and helps customers in their shopping. Shopping cart software makes it easy for the customers to search, browse, select, and order your products.

If a customer likes a product, they can put the product in a virtual shopping cart. After they have selected all the products, they can pay for it. These software packages work seamlessly with "SSL" secure servers for greater security; customers are unlikely to give their credit card numbers online without such security.

At any point, the customer can see a running total of the amount spent, including taxes and shipping, as well as special sales discounts. It is easy for the customer to remove an item from the shopping cart at any time. It is also possible to "pause" your shopping and continue it at a later time and in a different session. Recently "storefront" software packages with integrated shopping cart programs have appeared. When a company offers a large number of products, customers should easily be able to search and find what they need. Typically a sophisticated navigation system is needed. While it is possible to have a set of related products on a single page, frequently each page contains only one product.

The storefront software can keep track of customer information, including home mailing address. The address information can then be used to calculate sales tax, if any, as well as shipping costs. Some programs can help customers more accurately determine shipping costs by connecting with United Parcel Service's (UPS) Quick Cost Calculator at www.ups.com.

The storefront software automatically generates a receipt and an order confirmation and emails it to customers. The storefront software offers the merchant several advantages. A successful store is always innovating and changing. Storefront software packages allow merchants to quickly add or delete products. Prices can be changed and promotions can be organized. Discounts can be given to a certain set of customers. Stocked out items can be temporarily hidden. More sophisticated packages offer the ability to include extra information, such as the size, color, or model type. Each combination of the product variety generally has a unique "SKU" number for tracking inventory and fulfilling orders. Some items can be placed on sale. The data from the storefront software can be integrated into a company's accounting and inventory system.

The membership feature of storefront software packages allows merchants to keep track of prospective and actual customers. Prospective customers may be offered a special discount if they provide basic information about themselves. Such customers may then be emailed information about special sales and promotions. It is also possible to track the shopping and browsing habits of customers. This information may be used to offer discounts to special customers. The first time a prospective customer visits, the server can send a cookie to the browser to help you identify the visitor in subsequent visits. A major benefit of customer tracing is the ability to cross sell.

Most storefront software offers a variety of reports and statistics. They can generate reports on products that were viewed, or the products that were actually purchased. It may also give you information about the path taken by most customers in your site.

Internet Malls

Malls on the Internet are gaining some popularity. Internet malls are similar to real world malls. Several shops feed customers to each other. Economies of scale are often possible, especially in promoting and advertising the mall web site. Some Internet malls charge a percentage of the sale transaction. There are many free malls that will create a link to your site. Many malls with their own shopping cart programs will not reveal the email of the purchaser. Many malls limit the ability of merchants to advertise on their own, and require shoppers to enter the mall's main entrance.

Selecting an Internet Service Provider

To publish web pages, you need a web server. Your customers' browsers will be requesting files from your web server. Web servers and browsers communicate using the Hyper Text Transfer Protocol (HTTP). Web servers also perform some basic file management functions and maintain a log of activities.

It is possible to set up your own server or use an Internet Service Provider (ISP) to host your web pages. The cost of setting up a private server as well as technically maintaining it makes it difficult for most businesses. The greatest expense typically is the communication charges for obtaining adequate bandwidth.

A commercial ISP is often the best choice for many businesses. However, ISPs sometimes have restrictions. For example, you may not have the ability to run Common Gateway Interface (CGI) scripts which are essential for interactivity. Disk space may be limited. Most ISPs charge a flat monthly fee. However, if your site is very popular or you have web pages that consume a lot of disk space as well as bandwidth, you may be asked to pay additional fees. A major advantage of using ISP is access to their technological expertise. ISPs have professional site administrators to make sure there are no technical problems. Most ISPs offer "virtual hosting." This allows you to have your own domain name rather than use your ISP's domain name with a subdirectory designating your site. Virtual hosting is essential from a marketing perspective.

Geographic restrictions should not be a factor when selecting an ISP. An ISP anywhere in the world can host your site. US businesses will probably want a US-based ISP; overseas Internet connections tend to be typically slower. Many non-US businesses also use a US-based ISP. You can get local dial-up Internet access to save on toll calls and send files to the ISP hosting your site using File Transfer Protocol (FTP). The primary aim should be to select an ISP that provides the best service as well as price. ISPs offer a range of services as well as prices.

It is essential to exercise care when selecting an ISP. Before committing to any ISP, you should visit their customers' web sites. See how fast the pages download and whether it is possible to get to their web site without difficulty. It is easy for anyone to start an ISP business. Some ISPs may be pursuing this as a sideline business and working only on a part-time basis. Their prices are usually significantly cheaper. However, there are significant drawbacks. Such companies may not have full technical expertise. They may not have the hardware capability that you need. Technical support and customer service is generally lacking. It is dangerous to set up a business web site with someone that does not provide appropriate technical support. Such ISPs are also unlikely to be able to handle the volume of hits generated by a successful web site.

The larger ISPs may charge more, but they normally provide adequate technical support. Such ISPs have a large number of customers and may not be as eager for your business as smaller ISPs. They usually have the latest hardware and offer fast connection to the Internet. Larger ISPs are the only choice if your site generates a lot of hits. Such ISPs offer 24 hour technical support. They have redundant connections to the Internet. Many provide mirror sites. Their reliability tends to be exceptional.

Many local dial-up Internet access providers also host web pages for businesses. Sometimes, these ISPs do not understand the needs of businesses. It is generally safer to use an ISP that specializes in web hosting and not providing dial-up access. The lack up dial-up connections generally means that the bandwidth is not compromised by their Internet users.

When selecting an ISP, inquire about the following:

- How many businesses are hosted by each of the ISP's computers?
- How much space is assigned for web pages? Are email and log files counted towards assigned space?
- Is virtual hosting possible?
- Is access provided to the CGI bin directory?
- How many email addresses are allowed? Can you set up multiple "aliases?" Can different aliases be forwarded to multiple email addresses?
- Is it possible to have multiple Post Office Protocol (POP) email boxes?
- What type of a contract will have to be signed? How long is the commitment period? Can you easily leave the ISP if you are not satisfied?
- What are the hours technical support staff are available?
- Does the ISP offer mailing list management programs?
- Does the ISP offer autoresponders to automatically respond to e-mail messages?
- What type of statistical data about web visitors is provided by the ISP?
- Does the ISP provide SSL security for credit card transaction?
- Who are some of your current customers?
- How slow is the site during peak hours?

▶ How long has the ISP been in business?

▶ Are there many complaints against the ISP? (Check with Better Business Bureau.)

You should check references when selecting an ISP. Ask the ISP's customers about the quality of service. Is the ISP reliable? How frequently has the system of the ISP been down and for how long? How long have they been with the ISP? How accessible and knowledgeable is the technical support provided by the ISP? Would you recommend the ISP?

It is essential to have your own domain name. This way you always have the option to transfer to another ISP if your ISP fails to meet your expectations.

The List™ at www.thelist.com is an excellent place to search for ISPs. You can locate ISPs by:

▶ area code,

▶ country code,

▶ in the United States,

▶ in Canada.

Web directories are sites that organize other sites by categories, such as Computers, Business, Sports, etc. Each category has sub-categories and sub-categories may have additional levels. This allows the web user to find information on a particular topic more easily.

e-Commerce Success Factors

The following is a summary of major ingredients that lead to a successful e-commerce..

▶ **Selection and Value** – attractive product selections, competitive prices, satisfaction guarantees, and customer support after the sale

▶ **Performance and Service** – fast, easy navigation, shopping, and purchasing, and prompt shipping and delivery

▶ **Look and Feel** – attractive web storefront, website shipping areas, multimedia product catalog pages, and shopping features

▶ **Advertising and Incentives** – targeted web page advertising and e-mail promotions, discounts and special offers, including advertising at affiliate sites

▶ **Personal Attention** – personal web pages, personalized product recommendations, Web advertising and e-mail notices, and interactive support for all customers

▶ **Community Relationships** – virtual communities of customers, suppliers, company representatives, and others via newsgroups, chat rooms, and links to related sites

▶ **Security and Reliability** – security of customer information and website transactions, trustworthy product information, and reliable order fulfillment.

CHAPTER 6

Electronic Data Interchange and XML

EC involves the electronic exchange of data between trading partners using technologies such as email, faxes, electronic funds transfer (EFT), and electronic data interchange (EDI). For example, a buyer's computer will issue a purchase order to a seller's computer. EDI was developed to enhance JIT inventory management. The advantages of EDI include reduction of clerical errors, speed, elimination of repetitive clerical tasks, and elimination of document preparing, processing, and mailing costs.

EDI is a critical part of electronic commerce. It allows the trading partners to exchange data in a faster, cheaper, and more accurate way. Electronic Data Interchange (EDI) involves the exchange of electronic messages between trading partners. The messages are structured in a prearranged format to facilitate automatic computer processing. The electronic messages generally result in a legally binding contract.

EDI is playing a vital role in facilitating electronic commerce. Several factors, including advances in hardware, software, and communication technologies, are increasing the role of EDI in business transactions. Trade agreements such as the NAFTA and economic union of Europe have lifted trade barriers and EDI is a tool businesses need to remain competitive. The boundaries between manufacturers, suppliers, and customers tend to disappear when using EDI. The expectation for growth in EDI applications is very high.

EDI entails the exchange of common business data converted into standard message formats. Thus, two crucial requirements are that the participants agree on transaction formats and that translation software be developed to convert messages into a form understandable by other companies. Thus, if one company changes its software, its trading partners must also do so.

EDI is a fast, inexpensive, and secure way of transmitting purchase orders, invoices, shipping notices, and other business documents. There is no need to issue purchase orders, inquire about shipments or order status, or to write checks or transfer funds. While EDI involves the exchange of electronic messages, it is not the same as sending faxes or email messages or sharing files through a network, a modem, or a bulletin board. These do not satisfy the definition of EDI because they do not use standardized machine processable structured data formats. Non-EDI file transfers require the computer applications of trading partners to generate files in an identical format. EDI, however, does not require the trading partners to have identical computer processing systems. When the sender sends a document, the EDI translation software automatically converts the proprietary format into an agreed upon standard. When the receiver gets the document, the receiver's EDI translation software automatically changes the standard format into the receiver's proprietary format. *Note:* EDI for business documents between unrelated parties has the potential to increase the risk of unauthorized third-party access to systems because more outsiders will have access to internal systems.

Integrated EDI saves re-keying of data. Data from documents such as purchase orders is automatically integrated into a company's computer system. The exchange of data using the EDI process is invisible to the end user. EDI increases the productivity of trading partners. It reduces the cycle time of data interchange, eliminates paper work, reduces postage costs, and improves accuracy. It is easy to implement Just-In-Time Inventory management for faster and better service. EDI improves working capital management by reducing investment in inventories and receivables and by providing better control over payables. The amount of lead time to respond to customers' requests is greatly reduced.

For electronic commerce to succeed, trading partners must have trust in data generated through EDI. Special controls are essential in an EDI environment. Paper based audit techniques are ineffective. Computerized tests should be used to ensure that the electronic records are correct. For example, tests could be performed to check whether the number sequence continuity of the sales invoice is maintained. If it is not maintained, the computer can trace the gaps and generate a variance report for the auditor. The auditor, however, cannot rely only on the computer. EDP auditors need to ensure that computer programs are properly written and unauthorized alterations are not made.

EDI has been under development in the U.S. in one form or another since the mid-1960s. Still EDI is in the very early stages in most companies. Companies have been using Value Added Networks (VANs) to store and forward data. Using VANs, the trading partners do not need to have direct connections in order to send or receive the data.

The sender's computer can transmit the data to a VAN and the VAN will transmit the data to the receiving trading partner's computer system. VANs, however, are proprietary and relatively expensive. In contrast, the Internet provides a relatively low-cost method for retailers to communicate, without diminishing the major benefits of VANs.

The use of the Internet for EDI will reduce the cost of transmitting data considerably. However, because the Internet is open, special security precautions must be taken. The Internet traffic flows over circuits operated by various different government, academic, and private organizations and encryption is required for security purposes.

Implementing EDI

Before EDI is implemented, a determination should be made about which departments and functions will benefit from the change. Implementation generally involves:
- redesigning and simplifying the information flows
- converting the manual paper based system to an electronic system
- using the information flows in innovative and creative ways

EDI should be viewed as a strategic business tool. The paper system should not simply be replaced with an electronic system without rethinking and redesigning it. Benefits of a properly implemented EDI include:
- reduction in paper transactions and paper handling
- reduction in clerical costs, including hiring fewer personnel
- lower investments in inventory and receivables
- fewer processing errors
- faster trading cycle
- reduction in filing and storage costs
- reduction in postage expenses
- greater confidence in data
- improved relations with customers and suppliers
- ability to utilize techniques such as Just-in-Time manufacturing.
- improved sales productivity
- greater competitive position
- less reliance on human interpretation of data
- better record-keeping
- faster and more accurate filling of orders
- faster billing
- better information for decision making
- enhanced image

EDI technology is well established. Most businesses can't afford to ignore EDI. Most larger organizations already utilize EDI. Other organizations may not yet have implemented

EDI due to financial considerations. However, with the increased use of the Internet for EDI, financial considerations are no longer likely to be a significant barrier. EDI is likely to gain greater popularity. EDI will be needed to attract and retain customers.

Senior Management

Senior management's support is essential in implementing EDI. Developing an EDI system, especially a large and complex one, is costly and timely. Hardware and software for EDI has to be purchased. There are charges for third party networks. There are ongoing costs for maintaining and supporting the EDI system. Senior management is concerned not only with financial resources, but also with the availability of technical personnel and the effect of EDI on relations with trading partners. Therefore, no action should be taken unless a formal commitment has been obtained from top management. The management should be educated in the benefits of EDI. Sufficient resources, both human and financial, are needed for a successful implementation and it is not possible to get these resources without senior management's commitment.

Implementation Costs

The up-front costs of implementing an EDI system can range from a few thousand to several million dollars. Both the variable and fixed costs should be determined. The accounting department can play a critical role in preparing accurate financial projections for cost/benefit analysis. A comprehensive cost-benefit analysis considers the time value of money. The costs and benefits of a new EDI system are likely to extend to several years. For smaller EDI systems, where the costs and benefits do not extend beyond a few years, time value of money may be ignored. However, larger EDI systems may take several years and discounted cash flow analysis should be performed. The tax effects of investing in EDI should be considered. There may be an investment tax credit or it may be possible to use accelerated depreciation methods. Since the computations may be complicated, many companies find hiring an external consultant to assist with cost-benefit analysis helpful.

Project Team

An EDI project team consisting of both line and staff functions should take charge of implementation. The EDI project team is responsible for planning the schedule and allocating necessary resources. Schedules should be realistic and should have been prepared using a participative process. The team provides overall guidance and a project leader should be selected for managing daily activities. Personnel from all departments affected by EDI should participate. Input should be obtained from end users. The purchasing and sales managers should actively participate in EDI decision making. Support from purchasing and sales departments, as well as accounting, finance, and information technology departments are essential. The project team should:

- study the existing information gathering system
- determine which areas, departments, or functions are likely to benefit from EDI
- prepare a rank ordered list in terms of functions most likely to benefit
- identify key trading partners
- prepare a cost of implementation report
- make a pilot implementation plan
- select a potential trading partner
- obtain agreement from a potential trading partner
- obtain agreement with trading partners on standards
- evaluate communication systems
- evaluate EDI translation software
- appraise results of pilot testing

The EDI project team might need several months to complete its analysis. Multi-divisional companies must decide if the EDI functions should be centralized or distributed to each division. A decision should be made about whether EDI should first be implemented on the purchases site or sales side. The overall corporate strategy must be considered. The EDI team should be responsible for developing a strategic plan, including the goals and objectives of implementing EDI. Realistic goals should be established. It should be possible to modify goals based upon changing market and financial needs. Periodically, progress in implementing EDI should be reviewed and monitored to ensure it is consistent with the long-term goals of the company. The responsibility of each team member should be clearly defined. The EDI project team should consider how personnel will be trained and educated in the new system. Special attention should be devoted to security considerations and the ability to audit the system. Legal issues in EDI tend to be complex and the legal department should play an integral role.

The EDI project team should conduct a comprehensive operational and financial analysis of the costs and benefits of EDI. Operational analysis involves studying existing business practices to determine where improvements may be warranted. For instance, the project team should consider how the data from free standing business applications may be integrated to reduce processing time. Operational analysis should help identify the strengths and weaknesses of existing business procedures. Areas that are suitable for EDI development should be identified. EDI should enhance information flow, not merely convert it from paper to electronic format. Operational analysis should help the team prioritize areas likely to benefit the most from EDI conversion. Financial analysis involves undertaking a cost/benefit analysis. How will the qualitative factors affect the company's revenues and expenses? Such analysis tends to be difficult since it may not be possible to quantify some of the costs and benefits. Effort should be made to quantify the benefits of the qualitative factors. Qualitative factors such as the following should be considered:

- How will the reliability of daily operations be affected?
- What productivity gains are expected?
- How will data integrity and quality be affected?
- Will decision making be facilitated at the company and between its trading partners?
- Will it provide the company with a competitive edge?

Feasibility

The company's existing system should be evaluated to determine if it can handle EDI directly. If major modifications are necessary, it is generally better to obtain a new system. Several factors should be considered in determining the feasibility of using EDI.

- Are there enough paper based transactions?
- Are there sufficient suppliers and/or customers willing to participate in EDI?
- Are key suppliers or customers insisting that you implement EDI?
- Is there a desire to reduce the number of personnel?
- What effect will EDI have on information systems management?

Selecting Trading Partners for Pilot Testing of EDI

A survey should be conducted to identify potential trading partners. In the survey, customers may be asked if they are already placing orders using EDI. If they are, what is the extent of their involvement with EDI? What percentage of orders are placed using EDI? How long have they been using EDI? If they are not already using EDI, they should be asked when they plan to start using EDI.

A determination should be made of the readiness of customers and suppliers to implement EDI. Which potential partners are:

- already involved with EDI?
- in the process of converting to EDI?
- not ready for EDI?

After evaluating potential trading partners, they should be rank ordered in term of suitability. Initially, the company may wish to work with a few or even a single partner as part of a pilot implementation. The aim of the pilot program is to identify potential problems. The pilot EDI program should be run concurrently with existing procedures. The feedback from the pilot program is used to assess system performance, capacity, and security. As the EDI system is used, the existing system may be slowly phased out.

Pilot Program

The pilot program will give better insight into the firm's ability to implement EDI and the related cost-benefit considerations. In a typical pilot test, an EDI application is built with a single or few trading partners to assess the ability to process daily transactions. The EDI transmissions are then monitored for performance and effectiveness. The EDI system is evaluated to determine whether it will satisfy current and projected future needs. System security and auditability are of prime importance.

Ideally, the trading partners used for pilot testing should already have experience with EDI. They should also have significant paper based transactions with your firm. Since errors are likely to happen in the initial stages, the trading partners' management should understand the risks and be willing to support your company's implementation of EDI. The responsibilities of the trading partners should be clearly defined. A plan should be formulated defining the types of transactions to be automated. Data integrity issues need to be addressed. Training and education about EDI should be provided to appropriate individuals.

Dynamic Environment

Businesses operate in an ever changing environment and the EDI implementation process must be dynamic. The EDI process should be modified on an ongoing basis according to company needs. The EDI system should be monitored to evaluate its strengths and weaknesses. Data accuracy and reliability are critical in earning and retaining user confidence in the EDI system. Further modifications will generally be necessary when additional customers and suppliers are added to the system.

Designing and Developing the EDI System

Three factors affect data flow in EDI systems:
- ▶ *EDI Standards and Conventions:* Standards are used to structure the data. Data is structured with respect to product description, code, price, as well as merchant information such as merchant name and address.

▶ *Translation Software:* The EDI translation software converts data into different formats seamlessly. It is capable of converting internal data to a standardized format for external use and converting external data for internal use.

▶ *Communication:* The communication structure enables the exchange of messages between trading partners. It is possible to exchange data using magnetic media, such as tapes and discs. However, most data is exchanged on networks, including private networks, third party networks (VANs), and the Internet.

The five basic steps in exchanging data are as follows. Data is:

▶ extracted from the sender's internal computer applications

▶ converted to a standardized format using translation software

▶ transmitted using some type of communication media

▶ converted from the standardized format by the receiver's translating software

▶ imported into the receiver's computer applications

After reviewing the existing system, the requirements of the new EDI system should be determined. Attention should be given to auditing, security, and legal needs. The EDI system should be kept as simple as possible. While it is possible that a large, complex EDI system will serve the needs of companies, many companies either lack resources or simply do not need all the features of such a complex system. Extensive changes might be required in hardware and software. Information technology personnel with expertise in EDI may need to be recruited to develop and support the EDI system. Several software vendors provide customized EDI packages. For larger organizations, it is possible to develop EDI software.

There are two basic EDI design methods. The point to point EDI design is used where data is transferred electronically between trading partners, but is not processed automatically. The electronic message from the trading partners is printed upon receipt and processed manually. Re-keying of data is required under this system. There are no significant advantages to implementing such a system; in fact, a company is likely to incur extra costs by implementing such a system. The point to point EDI system is generally used only when a company is forced into EDI by a single or few customers or suppliers. This design may also be used during initial stages of converting to EDI, until a relationship is established with a significant number of trading partners.

The system to system design is used when the trading partners can be completely trusted. The trading partners' data is automatically processed directly into the company's applications. System security and data integrity is especially important; unauthorized users should not be able to edit files or make changes. Precautions need to be taken to avoid contamination of data files.

EDI Standards

EDI standards are needed to format electronic messages. EDI standards describe the rules or syntax that must be followed in creating an electronic message or document. Examples of electronic documents include purchase orders, invoices, and promotional information. The set of rules for formatting a specific electronic document is referred to as a transaction set. A transaction set is essentially the electronic equivalent of paper commercial documents. Directories refer to the message itself and its related components: segments, data elements and codes. A transaction set typically consists of several data segments. Data segments consist of several data elements, such as unit price or quantity.

Standards are needed to create EDI documents for accurate transmission of data between the trading partners. Several EDI standards are available, including:

- The ASC X12 standards developed by the ANSI (American National Standards Institute), also called ANSI X 12, is used predominantly in North America, Australia and New Zealand.
- The UNTDI is used primarily in Western Europe
- EDIFACT standard for international use
- NACHA (National Automated Clearing House Association) standards for banking transactions

The first three standards are used extensively by a variety of businesses. The format for these three standards is defined broadly. It has to meet the requirements of many diverse industries. Records are typically variable-length and allow optional fields. In contrast, proprietary EDI standards tend to be highly structured. The record length is generally fixed and little variation is allowed. Specific communication equipment and communication protocols are used. Many firms using proprietary formats developed earlier are now converting to generic standards.

The NACHA standards are a financial subset for electronic payments. They are used to transfer payments to trading partners using financial institutions. Electronic Funds Transfer (EFT) or Fedwire makes real-time transfer of financial information.

Several industries, such as aerospace, automotive, chemical, electrical and many others, have adapted the ASC X12 standards for their specific needs. Industry specific conventions should be used whenever possible. To keep track of changes, the ASC X12 standards have version and release numbers. The EDI standards are continuously evolving and changing. Changes in informational needs as well as changes in technology affect EDI standards. Revisions are published on a frequent basis. New standards are approved to meet changing needs. Your company's standards policy should be to support the most current version as well as a few prior versions, as appropriate. This gives trading partners a chance to upgrade without forcing anyone to comply in a short period of time. Without such a policy, all trading partners would have to upgrade simultaneously. This would create significant logistical problems. Each company may have hundreds or even thousands of trading partners and it is virtually impossible for everyone to upgrade simultaneously.

The United Nations-sponsored set of EDI standards are known as UN/EDIFACT (Electronic Data Interchange for Administration, Commerce and Transport). The EDIFACT standards are used extensively in Europe and Asia. EDIFACT was created by combining the best features of UNTDI and ANSI X.12. It was deemed essential that there be a common set of standards for the world; there should not be national or regional syntax standards. Many industries use only the EDIFACT.

Federal Government and EDI

The federal government is now using EDI to reduce paperwork and related costs, as well as enhance the efficiency of the procurement process. The executive branch agencies have been using EDI since 1993. The Federal Acquisition Streamlining Act (FASA) of 1994 requires that all governmental agencies use EDI. This means that only EDI capable merchants will be able to sell to the Department of Defense (DOD) and other civil agencies.

The Federal Acquisition Computer Network (FACNET) is used by FASA to refer to the system architecture. The FACNET system is intended to provide a "single face" to industry with most requirements to be enacted by 1999. The FACNET architecture has two network entry points (NEPs), with a third coming soon. In case of failure, two NEPs are used to provide redundancy. All EDI traffic must flow through these NEPs. A Department of Defense certified VAN provider must be used to access FACNET. The FACNET is used to enhance the acquisition process. The public can be informed of contracting opportunities. The government can receive solicitations as well as post contracting award notices. Businesses should be registered as trading partners with the government to remain competitive. For example, Request for Quotation documents may be transmitted by the government to all registered trading partners and bids may be sent by merchants.

Registration is used to inform the government of your intention to do business with it. Registration is performed using EDI. Each trading partner with the government is assigned a distinctive identification number. You are required to provide the following information:

- ▶ Company name
- ▶ Address
- ▶ Contact number such as the phone or fax number
- ▶ Taxpayer Identification Number (TIN)

- EDI point of contact
- Contractor Identification Numbers
- Commercial and Government Entity (CAGE) Code
- Data Universal Numbering System (DUNS)
- Standard Industrial Classifications (SIC)
- Version of ASC X12 standard

Value Added Networks (VANs)

While magnetic tapes or disks may be used to exchange data, most organizations utilize some type of a network. Magnetic media imposes several limitations. As the volume of transactions increases, data exchange using magnetic media become difficult. Magnetic media is not as timely. Exchanges between a large number of trading partners become complex and difficult to manage. Networks solve most of these problems; they can handle large transaction volume with many trading partners. Networks are timely; they can transmit business documents almost instantly. However, security concerns are greater with a network.

Private networks between trading partners tend to be expensive, especially if there are a large number of partners. Most businesses use VANs to communicate. VANs are similar to a combination of a telephone company and an electronic post office. VANs receive electronic documents, reads the addressing information, and forwards it to the recipient's mailbox. VANs provide a single channel to facilitate communication. A company only has to be concerned about its connection to the VAN. The VAN supports links to their networks. You don't have any responsibility for connections of your customers or suppliers. VANs providers possess the expertise and equipment necessary to communicate electronically.

Most VANs operate 24 hours a day. They route, store, and forward electronic messages. Most provide reliable connectivity and support various communication speeds and protocols. Security is maintained. Technical support is available. Audit trails are also maintained. Most VANs offer translation services.

While VANs are typically reliable, there is always a possibility of delayed or lost transmissions. VANs should provide a backup service to retrieve data. It is possible that your company will have to join more than one VAN. If you have several customers and suppliers, they may not all be using the same VAN. In the past, the various VANs were not connected to each other. Most networks support interconnections with each other. Joining one network gives you access not only to the VAN, but also all interconnected networks. Exchanging data on an interconnected network may mean a loss of audit trail. The audit trail is needed to ensure that a transaction can be traced from its source to its destination; it is used to verify that transactions are transmitted and processed correctly.

VANs have to maintain a high level of security. Department of Defense certified VANs are needed to do business with the government. The information transmitted over the networks contains sensitive business information. Most VANs require you to specify in advance the type of documents that may be transmitted electronically. Similarly, the receiver may have to specify the type of documents it will accept. The transmission will fail without consent by both trading partners. Most networks monitor the integrity of their transmissions to ensure the necessary EDI standards are being used. This checking allows re-transmission of lost data.

Most VANs offer some level of implementation assistance. They provide training and consulting services. The primary business of VANs is to process and transmit a large number of electronic business transactions. They may not be able to provide specific guidance on implementing EDI. Add-on services vary considerably among VANs. A key factor in selecting a VAN should be the number of trading partners connected with it. Some of the factors to consider in selecting a VAN are given in Exhibit 6.1.

Using The Internet for EDI

The Internet offers EDI users the possibility of greatly reducing their communication costs. Internet connections are typically significantly lower; a flat fee is charged for virtually unlimited connection time. In contrast, the connection costs for VANs are typically much higher and additional fees may also be charged. At present, the scope for EDI using the Internet is somewhat limited. However, over the next few years, the Internet may overtake traditional VANs.

There are several differences between the Internet and VANs. The Internet's only function is to provide a communications pipeline. VANs, however, provide not only the communications pipeline, but also several additional services essential to EDI, including but not limited to EDI security. ISPs do not offer many features such as:

- translation software
- user reports
- screening for type of messages
- screening for authorized trading partners
- checking to ensure that transmissions comply with standards
- non-delivery warning
- backup system

Customer support for EDI specific questions is not provided by Internet Service Providers (ISPs). This means that the ISP will not generally provide implementation assistance or train your employees or provide a technical support for EDI. Such customer services are routinely provided by VANs.

There are two basic ways the Internet can currently be used for EDI:

▶ *File Transfer Protocol (FTP):* The file transfer protocol is used to download files from the Internet. Using FTP application software, EDI files may be sent or retrieved. It is possible to automate the process. The sender can automatically convert application data into a standardized format and FTP the file to the recipient's computer. The recipient's computer automatically translates the FTP file for use in its application software. The FTP method is easy to use. However, file transfers using FTP do not provide security for sensitive data.

▶ *Email:* The sender can simply attach EDI files to an email message. The receiver retrieves the file from the email, translates it using appropriate translation software, and imports the data into application software. This approach, like FTP, does not provide data security. It is possible for email messages to get lost and not be delivered. To maintain reliability of the EDI system, it is essential for the parties to acknowledge receiving the email.

The World Wide Web (WWW) offers opportunities for partial EDI. WWW technology allows global access to all types of data including text, sound, and video. The primary reason for the popularity of the Internet has been the simplicity and adaptability of the Internet's open and standard protocols. It represents a major shift away from closed proprietary systems. Many businesses have opened virtual storefronts on the Internet. Customers can visit their electronic store, browse through their catalog, and place orders. The data inputted by the customers is captured for use by internal application software. The WWW does not result in a true EDI since customers have to physically key in the data at a business' web site; the input process at a business's web site is not currently automated.

The Intranet and the Extranet offer additional opportunities for EDI. Management may establish an Intranet and Extranet to improve operating efficiencies and productivity and to lower operating costs (e.g., distribution expenses), time, and errors. The Intranet is a network that serves the internal needs of a business. It is essentially a private Internet; it is an internal version of the Internet. Intranet users are able to access the Internet, but firewalls keep outsiders from accessing private and confidential data. It makes use of the infrastructure and standards of the Internet and World Wide Web using a TCP/IP based network. In an Intranet, one protocol connects all users to the Web server. Intranets run on standard protocols supported by any computer. Intranets use low-cost Internet tools and this allows you to cut costs, improve operational effectiveness, and gain a strategic advantage. Intranets are easy to install and offer tremendous flexibility.

The Extranet serves as a bridge between the public Internet and the private Intranet. The Extranet allows one to connect multiple organizations behind virtual

107

firewalls. These organizations can partner and share the network for transactions. For example, suppliers, distributors, contractors, customers and trusted others outside the organization can benefit from establishing an Extranet. The Internet is used to provide access to the public, whereas the Intranet serves the internal business. Extranets provide a critical link between these two extremes. Extranets are especially important because this is where the majority of business activity occurs. Extranets enable commerce through the Web at a very low cost and allow companies to maintain one-to-one relationships with their customers, members, staff and others.

Intranets and Extranets provide a communications platform. Intranets and Extranets provide the following applications:

- easy navigation (internal home page provides links to information)
- can integrate distributed computing strategy (localized web servers residing near the content author)
- rapid prototyping (can be measured in days or even hours in some cases)
- accessible by most computing platforms
- scaleable (start small, build as requirements permit)
- extensible to various media types (video, audio, interactive applications)
- can be tied into "legacy" information sources (databases, existing word processing documents, groupware databases)

The benefits of Intranets/Extranets are:

- inexpensive to start, requires minimal investment in dollars or infrastructure
- open platform architecture means large (and increasing) number of add-on applications
- a distributed computing strategy uses computing resources more effectively
- more timely and less expensive than traditional information (paper) delivery

The extranet may be viewed either as part of a company's Intranet that is accessible to other companies or as a collaborative Internet with other companies. The information on the Extranet may be restricted to the collaborating organizations or may be available publicly. To enhance security, privately owned or leased transmission lines may be used.

Extranets are extremely powerful. They support and streamline business processes across collaborating companies. Collaborating organizations can determine who has access to what information in the on-line transaction cycle. Efficiencies are achieved through economies of scale and other returns on investment for collaborating companies. Extranets are flexible, scaleable, portable, and extensible. They may be used to integrate across distributed, cross-platform and heterogeneous system environments. Extranets significantly reduce barriers to cross-organizational networking.

A proactive approach is required to implement an Extranet. While Extranets rely on simple Internet based technology, the process is not effortless. Users at all levels from collaborating organizations must actively participate in the process. Consensus by the organizations on a common goal is important. Information should be maintained, but not duplicated, by all the collaborating organizations. The interface should be simple. HTML forms can be used to submit or modify information on the Extranet. An Extranet Web committee may be established to make the system maintenance more cohesive and promote and facilitate the use of the Extranet. Proper planning should minimize any disruption from the implementation of an Extranet.

EDI for business documents between unrelated parties has the potential to increase the risk of unauthorized third-party access to systems because more outsiders will have access to internal systems. The more accessible a computer is, the more susceptible it is to attacks. When setting up an Intranet or Extranet, you want the advantages of an accessible computer but want to limit exposure to security attacks. One solution is the installation of a firewall. Firewalls are control devices that can be used to protect the company's Intranet from unauthorized access and misuse of the Intranet to alter accounting and financial information, theft of property, obtain confidential data, or commit other inappropriate or fraudulent acts.

A firewall limits access to selected "gateways." A gateway is a computer or a router that selectively passes information between the inside and outside networks. It rejects all incoming traffic not specifically directed to itself. A proxy server is a program that mediates application-specific traffic through the firewall. It makes secure access less difficult and generally has additional logging, user authentication, and protocol-specific security capabilities. You may build your own firewall or use an Internet Service Provider who provides the firewall and gateway service between your network and the Internet. Add-on security tools are available to restrict usage by users such as preventing them from performing certain acts or visualizing certain "restricted" data.

Electronic Contracting

EDI results in electronic contracting. Not all electronic messages, however, result in electronic contracting. For example, messages with purely informational content do not create an electronic contract. Inter-firm messages do not result in electronic contracts; the law generally distinguishes between intra-firm and inter-firm communications. Electronic contracting occurs routinely in business. Examples of electronic offer and acceptance include:

▶ purchase orders

- ▶ invoices
- ▶ payments
- ▶ solicitation and submission of bids
- ▶ filing documents electronically with government
- ▶ advertising of goods or services

Trading partner agreements or EDI agreements are essential in electronic contracting. These agreements:

- ▶ clarify each party's rights and obligations
- ▶ specify the risk and liability of each party
- ▶ help avoid misunderstandings

Trading partner agreements are only between the trading partners; they do not cover third parties, such as VANs. Several model trading partners agreements have been developed by the legal and EDI community (e.g., American Bar Association, EDI Council of Canada, etc.). Agreements have also been developed for specific industries and countries. Model agreements provide a fair and balanced contract. Most entities will want to modify model trading agreements to suit their specific needs. An agreement gives the parties the ability to legally enforce electronic contracts.

A trading partner agreement should include the intent of parties to transact electronically. It should specify whether all trade or a specific portion of the trade between the two parties is covered by the agreement. Offer and acceptance are essential in any contract. It should be clearly specified in advance which transaction sets will constitute a legally enforceable acceptance. There should be an understanding with respect to electronic payments for trade. The parties should acknowledge that they will not repudiate the validity, integrity or reliability of EDI transactions, and will consider it equivalent to paper based transactions.

An agreement should be reached on the time and place of receipt of EDI communications. There are several possibilities to consider. Receipt takes place when:

- ▶ message is sent by the sender's computer system
- ▶ message is received by the receiver's computer system
- ▶ message is received at the receiver's mailbox on a third party's (e.g., VAN) computer system
- ▶ acknowledgment of receipt is sent by the recipient
- ▶ acknowledgment of receipt is received by the original sender

Acknowledgments are typically used to verify communications. Acknowledgments provide proof about a transaction's integrity and authority. Cryptographic methods should be used whenever possible, especially when the authenticity of the transaction is critical. Sometimes electronic signatures are used to verify a message's integrity; typically, these signatures are cryptographically created. However, any type of a symbol or party's name may be considered sufficient as a signature for purposes of offer and acceptance. A signature does not have to be cryptographically enhanced. As long the EDI system is reliable and trustworthy, a non-cryptographic signature is deemed sufficient. The location of the signature in messages should be as uniform as possible and the location should be agreed upon in advance.

Security considerations should be given special attention when drafting a trading partners agreement. Security affects the integrity and reliability of transactions. Security provides confidence that transactions are authentic. Security is needed to ensure that the transactions remain confidential. An EDI system's security and trustworthiness are essential ingredients in determining whether electronic contracting is legally enforceable. From a legal perspective, trading agreements generally require *commercially reasonable security*. However, the definition of commercially reasonable security is quite vague. It differs from industry to industry; for example, a much higher level of security will be required in the banking industry. The trading partner agreement should discuss the responsibilities of each party. For instance, to what extent is one party responsible for ensuring the security of its trading partner. Or, what actions will be taken in the event of a security breach.

Basic security risks in EDI include:
- access violations
- message modifications
- interruptions or delays
- message rerouting
- message repudiation

Passwords are frequently used to limit access. Without access controls, an unauthorized individual could initiate a transaction by pretending to be an authorized trading partner. Fictitious purchase orders may be sent or fictitious payments may be made. The reliability and integrity of the EDI system breaks down without appropriate access controls. Greater security is achieved by combining different access control techniques. Most commonly used access controls are techniques based upon:
- something a person knows, such as a password
- something a person possesses, such as magnetic cards or electronic keys
- some unique attribute of a person, such as fingerprints, voice prints, and retinal patterns

Unauthorized individuals may intentionally modify electronic messages. Messages may also be modified unintentionally through hardware, software or transmission error. Authentication of messages is a major concern, especially with respect to repudiation of a transaction. To minimize the risk of repudiation, irrevocable proof, such as a digital signature, may be used.

Managing Electronic Records

There should be a written policy of electronic records management. A record needs to be kept of each transaction among trading partners. Records management is necessary for auditing and governmental regulation purposes. Maintenance of audit trails is essential to the audit process. The Foreign Corrupt Practices Act (FCPA) applies to all publicly held companies and requires certain controls to be maintained to ensure transactions are executed with management's authorization and that appropriate records are kept. Similarly, financial and tax records need to be maintained to comply with the Internal Revenue Service (IRS) requirements. Records must be retained as long as they are "material." For tax purposes, the minimum time period is at least three years. Policies should be in place to reduce risk to electronic records. Risk is normally reduced by using appropriate controls. It is possible to reduce risk further by using cryptographic techniques and trusted entities.

Maintenance of audit trails tends to be more difficult in an electronic environment. The electronic nature of transactions does not result in a visible trail as it does in a paper based environment. For instance, a physical purchase order is prepared, typically in triplicate, in a paper based system. At each stage of a paper based system, paper work is done and a physical trail is established. Such a trail is normally lacking in electronic transactions. Computer software should be specifically designed to provide an audit trail. Most commercially prepared software packages have at least some type of audit trail capability.

Audit trail maintenance is especially important in an EDI environment. EDI transactions go through several systems. Electronic records and audit trail must be maintained by application software. Any data that is used for EDI needs to be translated into a standardized format; the translation software must maintain the audit trail. Any communication that is sent over the network must be accounted for by communication software. Data is then translated into an internal format by the recipients translation software; again audit trail must be kept. Finally, the data is used by the recipient's application software. In an EDI environment, a weakness in any system can create problems not just for a single entity, but also its trading partners. Therefore, each function at each stage should be reviewed and appropriate controls incorporated.

Exhibit 6.1: Factors to Consider in Selecting a VAN

Here are some of the factors you should consider when selecting a VAN. This list provides questions to ask about each VAN for use in your general evaluation.

Experience

1. How long has the VAN been in business?
2. How many customers does the VAN serve?
3. Is the VAN making a profit?
4. Will the VAN provide a list of references that can be checked?

Customer Service

1. Is customer service available 24 hours a day, seven days a week?
2. How long does it take customer service or technical support to respond to a call for help?
3. Does the VAN provide start-up support, as well as ongoing support after my first trading partner is established?

Business Service

1. If one of my trading partners is on the VAN and I want to begin exchanging documents, how long does it take to establish a connection with that trading partner?
2. If one of my trading partners is on a different VAN and I want to begin exchanging documents, how long does it take to establish a connection with that trading partner?
3. Can I establish the relationship myself, or do I need to call the VAN customer service to establish the relationship?
4. Will this VAN reach all my trading partners, or is there a need to subscribe to others?
5. How frequently are messages/transactions forwarded by the VAN from its network to the trading partner's network?
6. How long does the VAN retain transactions in a business' mailbox awaiting retrieval?
7. Does the VAN offer "bulletin board" services? Access to business databases? Profiling of business transactions?
8. What kind of report and billing data will be received? (number of transmissions, minutes of connection time, number of logons and failed logons?)
9. What kinds of audit trail and usage reports are available?
10. Does the VAN allow or provide for selective browse/download of electronic bid boards for RFPs and ITBs?
11. Does the VAN provide choices of translation software or services? If so, what are they?

Connectivity

1. I plan to connect with the VAN using:
   - ▶ An asynchronous modem on a personal computer
   - ▶ A bisynchronous modem
   - ▶ A dedicated leased line
2. Which of these does the network support?
3. Is the dial-up number a local number?
4. If not local, is it toll-free?

Back Up/Disaster Recovery

1. Has the VAN ever been "out of service"? If so, for what length of time?
2. Is a back-up system available?
3. Does the VAN keep an archive of the data it receives?
4. Can I request retransmission of data?
5. Where is the archived data stored?
6. How long does it take to retrieve it?
7. Does the VAN have a disaster recovery plan? Can I get a copy?
8. What kind of back-up systems does the VAN have for its phone lines and power supply?
9. In the event of a system failure, how long does it take before back-up systems are activated?
10. Who is liable for lost transmission data?

Security

1. What security arrangements will be used (passwords, automatic callback, etc)?
2. What measures does the network take to prohibit unauthorized access of my data?
3. What compliance checking system will be used to ensure data integrity?

Price Structure

Compare the costs VANs charge for EDI communications services. VAN pricing can be difficult to understand. Make sure you understand all charges from each VAN.

1. What is the price structure (start-up costs and ongoing costs)?
2. Is there a one-time initialization fee? How much is it?
3. Are there annual fees? How much are they?
4. Are there monthly mailbox fees? How much are they?
5. Are there annual line access fees? How much are they?
6. Are there different fees for prime time hours and non-prime time hours?

7. What are the prime-time hours and non-prime time hours?
8. What are the per document costs during prime time and non-prime time for the following?
   a. Send document
   b. Send characters (per 1000 characters)
   c. Send line-access fee if any (per 1000 characters)
   d. Receive document
   e. Receive characters (per 1000 characters)
   f. Receive line-access fee if any (per 1000 characters)
9. Are there volume discounts?

Exhibit 6.2: Acquiring EDI Hardware

Some of the factors to consider in acquiring hardware are as follows:
- Will the hardware satisfy the EDI requirements for the company and its trading partners?
- Will it be compatible with translation software?
- Will the hardware meet the projected needs of transaction volume?
- Will the storage space be sufficient?
- How many concurrent users can the hardware accommodate?
- Will the hardware be compatible with communication software?
- How much will the hardware cost?
- How much technical support is provided by the vendor?

Exhibit 6.3: Purchasing EDI Software

EDI software performs three essential functions:
- encodes outgoing data into a standardized format
  - decodes incoming data into internal format
  - dials the trading partner or communication network and sends or receives the formatted data

The software plays a critical role in the effectiveness of an EDI system. It is possible to either purchase or develop EDI translation software or use the VAN's translation software. The EDI software should:
- be easy to use and install
- offer the ability to create or modify data input screens
- allow for customization of output reports
- provide reporting of inbound/outbound transaction sets
- have the ability to create or modify routines for customized operations

- provide error reports
- be used to allow connection to multiple VANs
- guide the users when processing electronic data
- have the capability to convert data into several different formats
- offer security features
- offer selective accessibility using passwords
- maintain an audit trail
- have controls to ensure all transactions have been properly accounted
- be flexible and customizable
- run on the company's hardware
- permit batch transmissions
- offer scheduling flexibility
- support multiple versions of ASC X12 standards
- offer automated archiving and purging capability
- provide for automatic recover and restart
- allow for expandability based on future needs
- contain clear documentation
- offer context-sensitive help
- be competitively priced
- be supported adequately by the vendor, including training or consulting services
- provide for a number of installations (how many companies have previously implemented the software)

eXtensible Markup Language (XML)

The Extensible Markup Language (XML) is new technology to facilitate Internet based EDI. XML uses tags to indicate data values in a document. The tags can be defined on the basis of a document, application, or industry. They may also be defined on a global basis. XML offers great flexibility. It allows XML to mimic other proprietary or standard data formats making transfers easier. The data element in XML is similar to other markup languages such as HTML. There is a start tag, data, and end tag. A tag is a notation used to define a data element for display or other purposes.

XML has the potential to improve the efficiency of supply chain processes and activities. Many believe it will eventually replace EDI. Exhibit 4 lists some work done that is underway on XML standards in various industries.

Exhibit 6.4: XML Industry Standards

Industry	Example XML Standards
Banking	Bank Internet Payment System (BIPS); Financial Services Technology Consortium (FSTC)
Automotive	Society of Automotive Engineers
Insurance	ACORD: Property and Casualty
Real Estate	OpenMLS: Real Estate Listing Management System
Human Resources	HR-XML Consortium
Accounting	American Institute of Certifies Public Accountants: Extensible Financial Reporting Markup Language (EFRML)

Exhibit 6.5: Sources of EDI and XML Information

- CommerceNet (www.commerce.net)
- Data Interchange Standards Association (DISA) (www.disa.org)
- Department of Defense Business Transformation Office (www.dod.mil/dbt)
- Federal EDI Secretariat(http://fedebiz.disa.mil)
- FedWorld (www.fedworld.gov)
- General Services Administration (www.gsa.gov)
- Government Printing Office (www.gpoaccess.gov/index.html)
- World Wide Web Consortium (W3C) (www.w3.org)

CHAPTER 7

Electronic Banking and Payments

Electronic Banking and Payments are an integral part of Electronic Commerce. Electronic Commerce covers a very wide area of business. Automation of business transactions is the primary goal of electronic commerce. Business to business and individual to business transactions, online payments for services and goods, electronic bills payment, personal banking, and delivery of information are among the many other features of electronic commerce. Electronic Commerce covers improving the quality of service for online selling of products and information via the Internet, the telephone and private digital networks.

The most fundamental view of electronic commerce for business is effectively interacting customers and business partners. Exhibit 7.1 shows this relationship.

Exhibit 7.1

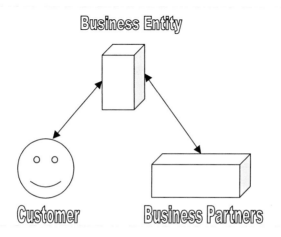

Electronic Funds Transfer (EFT) Systems

Electronic funds transfer (EFT) systems are a major form of electronic commerce systems in banking and retailing industries. EFT systems use a variety of information technologies to capture and process money and credit transfers between banks and businesses and their customers. EFT transaction costs are lower than for manual systems because documents and human intervention are eliminated from the transactions process. Competition has been a strong motivator in the financial services industry in the development of EFT systems, which are an application of EDI. Furthermore, containing costs in a highly competitive industry can be aided by leveraging information technology. Finally, advances in information technology, especially the wide acceptance of telecommunications standards and protocols, have made EFT systems possible. However, unauthorized access to money transfer activities or data is an inherent and unique risk of EFT systems. An unauthorized person may attempt to read, alter, or delete information in data files or to enter authorized fund transfers. Hence, in the financial services industry, protection of confidential customer transactions is especially important. Moreover, unauthorized transfers subject a financial institution to a direct risk of serious loss. The major requirement of Electronic Fund Transfer is real-time payment.

Online Payment Basics

User interaction is the most distinguished feature of the modern day electronic payment system. Earlier electronic payment systems did not (and could not) allow end-user interaction, thereby increasing the cost of payment and the time for payment completion. Today, four basic ways to pay for purchases dominate both traditional and electronic business-to-consumer commerce. Cash, checks, credit cards, and debit cards account for more than 90 percent of all consumer payments in the United States. A small but growing percentage of consumer payments are made by electronic transfer. The most popular consumer electronic transfers are automated payments of auto loans, insurance payments, and mortgage payments made from consumers' checking accounts.

Credit cards are by far the most popular form of consumer electronic payments online. Recent surveys have found that more than 85 percent of worldwide consumer Internet purchases are paid for with credit cards. In the United States, the proportion is about 96 percent.

Another payment medium is limited-use scrip. Scrip is digital cash minted by a company instead of by a government. Most scrip cannot be exchanged for cash; it must be exchanged for goods or services by the company that issued the scrip. Scrip is like a gift certificate that is good at more than one store. In the early days of the Web, many experts predicted that scrip would become a popular way of making payments for consumer goods and services online. Unfortunately for many investors and at least two companies, this turned out not to be true.

Payment Cards

Businesspeople often use the term payment card as a general term to describe all types of plastic cards that consumers (and some businesses) use to make purchases. The main categories of payment cards are credit cards, debit cards, and charge cards.

Payment Cards:

▶ Credit card: Has a spending limit based on the user's credit history; a user can pay off the entire credit card balance or pay a minimum amount each billing period.

▶ Debit card: Removes the amount of the sale from the cardholder's bank account and transfers it to the seller's bank account.

▶ Charge card: Carries no spending limit, and the entire amount charged to the card is due at the end of the billing period.

Advantages and Disadvantages of Payment Cards

Payment cards have several features that make them an attractive and popular choice with both consumers and merchants in online and offline transactions. For merchants, payment cards provide fraud protection. When a merchant accepts payment cards for online payment or for orders placed over the telephone - called card not present transactions because the merchant's location and the purchaser's location are different - the merchant can authenticate and authorize purchases using a payment card processing network. For U.S. consumers, payment cards are advantageous because the Consumer Credit Protection Act limits the cardholder's liability to $50 if the card is used fraudulently. Once the cardholder notifies the card's issuer of the card theft, the cardholder's liability ends. Frequently, the payment card's issuer waives the $50 consumer liability when a stolen card is used to purchase goods.

Perhaps the greatest advantage of using payment cards is their worldwide acceptance. Payment cards can be used anywhere in the world, and the currency conversion, if needed, is handled by the card issuer. For online transactions, payment cards are particularly advantageous. When a consumer reaches the electronic checkout, he or she enters the payment card number and his or her shipping and billing information in the appropriate fields to complete the transaction. The consumer does not need any special hardware or software to complete the transaction.

Payment cards have one significant disadvantage for merchants when compared to cash. Payment card service companies charge merchants per-transaction fees and monthly processing fees. These fees can add up, but merchants view them as a cost of doing business. Any merchant that does not accept payment cards for purchases risks losing a significant portion of sales to other merchants that do accept payment cards. The consumer pays no direct transaction-based fees for using payment cards, but the prices of goods and services are slightly higher than they would be in an environment free of payment cards. Most consumers also pay an annual fee for credit cards and charge cards. This annual fee is much less common on debit cards.

Payment Acceptance and Processing

Most people are familiar with the use of payment cards: In a physical store, the customer or a sales clerk runs the card through the online payment card terminal and the card account is charged immediately. The process is slightly different on the Internet, although the purchase and charge processes follow the same rules. Payment card processing has been made easier over the past two decades because Visa and MasterCard, along with MasterCard's international affiliate, MasterCard International (formerly known as Europay), have implemented a single standard for the handling of payment card transactions called the EMV standard (EMV is derived from the names of the companies: Europay, MasterCard, and Visa).

Steps Followed by Payment Card Transactions

▷ The merchant authenticates the payment card to ensure it is valid and not stolen.

▷ The merchant checks with the payment card issuer to ensure that credit or funds are available and puts a hold on the credit line or the funds needed to cover the charge.

▷ Settlement occurs, usually a few days after the purchase, which means that funds travel between banks and are placed into the merchant's account.

Electronic Cash

Although credit cards dominate online payments today, electronic cash shows promise for the future. Gartner, Inc. estimates that electronic cash will be used in more than 60 percent of all online transactions by 2009. Electronic cash (also called e-cash or digital cash) is a general term that describes any value storage and exchange system created by a private (nongovernmental) entity that does not use paper documents or coins and that can serve as a substitute for government-issued physical currency. A significant difference between electronic cash and scrip is that electronic cash can be readily exchanged for physical cash on demand. Because electronic cash is issued by private entities, there is a need for common standards among all electronic cash issuers so that one issuer's electronic cash can be accepted by another issuer. This need has not yet been met. Each issuer has its own standards and electronic cash is not universally accepted, as is government-issued physical currency.

Electronic Cash

▶ *Micropayments and Small Payments:* Internet payments for items costing from a few cents to approximately a dollar are called micropayments. Micropayment champions see many applications for such small transactions, such as paying 5 cents for an article reprint or 25 cents for a complicated literature search. However, micropayments have not been implemented very well on the Web yet.

▶ *Privacy and Security of Electronic Cash*: Electronic cash should have two important characteristics in common with physical currency. First, it must be possible to spend electronic cash only once, just as with traditional currency. Second, electronic cash ought to be anonymous, just as hard currency is.

▶ *Holding Electronic Cash: Online and Offline Cash*: Online cash storage means that the consumer does not personally possess electronic cash. Instead, a trusted third party (an online bank) is involved in all transfers of electronic cash and holds the consumers' cash accounts. Offline cash storage is the virtual equivalent of money kept in a wallet. The customer holds it, and no third party is involved in the transaction. Protection against fraud is still a concern, so either hardware or software safeguards must be used to prevent fraudulent or double-spending.

Advantages and Disadvantages of Electronic Cash

For the most part, electronic cash transactions are more efficient (and therefore less costly) than other methods, and that efficiency should foster more business, which eventually means lower prices for consumers. Transferring electronic cash on the Internet costs less than processing credit card transactions. Conventional money exchange systems require banks, bank branches, clerks, automated teller machines, and an electronic transaction system to manage, transfer, and dispense cash. Operating this conventional money exchange system is expensive.

Electronic cash transfers occur on an existing infrastructure - the Internet - and through existing computer systems. Thus, the additional costs that users of electronic cash must incur are nearly zero. Because the Internet spans the globe, the distance that an electronic transaction must travel does not affect cost. When considering moving physical cash and checks, distance and cost are proportional – the greater the distance that the currency has to go, the more it costs to move it. However, moving electronic currency from Los Angeles to San Francisco costs the same as moving it from Los Angeles to Hong Kong. Merchants can pay other merchants in a business-to-business relationship, and consumers can pay each other. Electronic cash does not require that one party obtain an authorization, as is required with credit card transactions.

Electronic cash does have disadvantages, and they are significant. Using electronic cash provides no audit trail. That is, electronic cash is just like real cash in that it cannot be easily traced. Because true electronic cash is not traceable, another problem arises: money laundering. Money laundering is a technique used by criminals to convert money that they have obtained illegally into cash that they can spend without having it identified as the proceeds of an illegal activity. Money laundering can be accomplished by purchasing goods or services with ill-gotten electronic cash. The goods are then sold for physical cash on the open market.

Providing Security for Electronic Cash

Cryptographic algorithms are the keys to creating tamper-proof electronic cash that can be traced back to its origins. A two-part lock provides anonymous security that also signals when someone is attempting to double-spend cash. When a second transaction occurs for the same electronic cash, a complicated process comes into play that reveals the identity of the original electronic cash holder. Otherwise, electronic cash that is used correctly maintains a user's anonymity. This double-lock procedure protects the anonymity of electronic cash users and simultaneously provides built-in safeguards to prevent double-spending.

Double-spending can neither be detected nor prevented with truly anonymous electronic cash. Anonymous electronic cash is electronic cash that, like bills and coins, cannot be traced back to the person who spent it. One way to be able to trace electronic cash is to attach a serial number to each electronic cash transaction. That way, cash can be positively associated with a particular consumer. That does not solve the double-spending problem, however. Although a single issuing bank could detect if two deposits of the same electronic cash are about to occur, it is impossible to ascertain who is at fault in such a situation - the consumer or the merchant. Of course, electronic cash that contains serial numbers is no longer anonymous, and anonymity is one reason to acquire electronic cash in the first place. Electronic cash containing serial numbers also raises a number of privacy issues, because merchants could use the serial numbers to track spending habits of consumers.

Electronic Cash Systems

Electronic cash has not been nearly as successful in the United States as it has been in Europe and Japan. In the United States, most consumers have credit cards, debit cards, charge cards, and checking accounts. These payment alternatives work well for U.S. consumers in both online and offline transactions. In most other countries of the world, consumers overwhelmingly prefer to use cash. Because cash does not work well for online transactions, electronic cash fills an important need for consumers in those countries as they conduct B2C electronic commerce. This type of need does not exist in the United States because U.S. consumers already use payment cards for traditional commerce, and these payment cards work well for electronic commerce.

Electronic Cash Systems

▶ *CheckFree*: The largest online bill processor in the world, provides online payment processing services to both large corporations and individual Internet users.

▶ Clickshare: An electronic cash system aimed at magazine and newspaper publishers.

▶ *InternetCash*: Provides electronic currency that is very similar to traditional cash. Similar to prepaid phone cards, the InternetCash cards come in denominations of $10, $20, $50, and $100.

▶ *PayPal*: Provides payment processing services to businesses and to individuals. PayPal earns a profit on the float, which is money that is deposited in PayPal accounts and not used immediately.

Electronic Wallets

As consumers are becoming more enthusiastic about online shopping, they have begun to tire of repeatedly entering detailed shipping and payment information each time they make online purchases. Filling out forms ranks high on online customers' list of gripes about online shopping. To address these concerns, many electronic commerce sites include a feature that allows a customer to store name, address, and credit card information on the site. However, consumers must enter their information at each site with which they want to do business. An electronic wallet (sometimes called an e-wallet), serving a function similar to a physical wallet, holds credit card numbers, electronic cash, owner identification, and owner contact information and provides that information at an electronic commerce site's checkout counter. Electronic wallets give consumers the benefit of entering their information just once, instead of having to enter their information at every site with which they want to do business.

Electronic wallets fall into two categories based on where they are stored. A server-side electronic wallet stores a customer's information on a remote server belonging to a particular merchant or wallet publisher. The main weakness of serverside electronic wallets is that a security breach could reveal thousands of users' personal information - including credit card numbers - to unauthorized parties. Typically, server-side electronic wallets employ strong security measures that minimize the possibility of unauthorized disclosure.

A client-side electronic wallet stores a consumer's information on his or her own computer. Many of the early electronic wallets were client-side wallets that required users to download the wallet software. This need to download software onto every computer used to make purchases is a chief disadvantage of client-side wallets. Server-side wallets, on the other hand, remain on a server and thus require no download time or installation on a user's computer. Before a consumer can use a server-side wallet on a particular merchant's site, the merchant must enable that specific wallet. Each wallet vendor must convince a large number of merchants to enable its wallet before it will be accepted by consumers. Thus, only a few server-side wallet vendors will be able to succeed in the market.

W3C Micropayment Standards Development Activity

Wallet information includes identification of the users and a complete record of their online purchasing activity. An alternative to having individual companies offer electronic wallet services is to have standards for electronic wallets built into the structure of the Web itself. With open standards, many different companies could offer electronic wallet services that would work on many different Web sites. This approach would distribute the information gathering and storage among a number of companies and thus reduce the risk of having one company in control of so much private information.

The World Wide Web Consortium (W3C) conducted an active standards development activity for micropayments in electronic commerce for several years. Although the activity has now been closed, the W3C Electronic Commerce Interest Group (ECIG) developed a set of standards called the Common Markup for Micropayment Per-Fee-Links before it ended its activities. The proposed ECIG micropayment links standard is a set of guidelines that provides an extensible and interoperable way to embed micropayment information in a Web page. An extensible system is one that developers can add to (or extend) without voiding any earlier work on the system.

The ECML Standard

The W3C initiative is not the only attempt to develop standards for the operation of electronic wallets. A consortium of several high-tech companies and credit card companies proposed an alternative standard that would replace the competing electronic wallet standards with a single standard. The consortium of companies, which includes America Online, Compaq, Dell, IBM, Microsoft, Visa U.S.A., and MasterCard, has agreed on a technology called ECML, or Electronic Commerce Modeling Language. Users can enter their credit card and address information once into an ECML-capable electronic wallet. Any existing wallet can be redesigned to follow the ECML standard, although none currently do. Users control access to their ECML electronic wallets, and the wallets will be accepted at all commerce sites if the consortium is successful in generating widespread acceptance. So far, several electronic wallet makers have accepted and implemented the standard. They include IBM, Microsoft, and Trintech.

Stored-Value Cards

Today, most people carry a number of plastic cards - credit cards, debit cards, charge cards, driver's license, health insurance card, employee or student identification card, and others. One solution that could reduce all those cards to a single plastic card is called a stored-value card.

A stored-value card can be an elaborate smart card with a microchip or a plastic card with a magnetic strip that records the currency balance. The main difference is that a smart card can store larger amounts of information and includes a processor chip on the card. The card readers needed for smart cards are different, too. Common stored-value cards include prepaid phone, copy, subway, and bus cards.

Stored-Value Cards
▶ *Magnetic strip card:* Holds a value that can be recharged by inserting it into the appropriate machines, inserting currency into the machine, and withdrawing the card; the card's strip stores the increased cash value. Magnetic strip cards are passive; that is, they cannot send or receive information, nor can they increment or decrement the value of cash stored on the card.
▶ *Smart card:* A stored-value card that is a plastic card with an embedded microchip that can store information. Credit, debit, and charge cards currently store limited information on a magnetic strip. A smart card can store about 100 times the amount of information that a magnetic strip plastic card can store. A smart card can hold private user data, such as financial facts, encryption keys, account information, credit card numbers, health insurance information, medical records, and so on.

Internet Technologies and the Banking Industry

Phishing expeditions, a technique for committing fraud against the customers of online businesses, can be launched against all types of online businesses, but are of particular concern to financial institutions because their customers expect a high degree of security to be maintained over the personal information and resources that they entrust to their online financial institutions.

The basic structure of a phishing attack is fairly simple. The attacker sends e-mail messages to a large number of recipients who might have an account at the targeted

Web site. The e-mail message tells the recipient that his or her account has been compromised and it is necessary for the recipient to log in to the account to correct the matter. The e-mail message includes a link that appears to be a link to the login page of the Web site. However, the link actually leads the recipient to the phishing attack perpetrator's Web site, which is disguised to look like the targeted Web site. The unsuspecting recipient enters his or her login name and password, which the perpetrator captures and then uses to access the recipient's account. Once inside the victim's account, the perpetrator can access personal information, make purchases, or withdraw funds at will.

CHAPTER 8

Network Security

Networks may be broadly classified as either wide area networks (WANs) or local area networks (LANs). Network security is needed for both LANs and WANs. The computers in a WAN may be anywhere from several miles to thousands of miles apart. In contrast, the computers in a LAN are usually closer together, such as in a building or a plant. Data switching equipment might be used in LANs, but not as frequently as it is in WANs.

On the Internet, security is needed to prevent unauthorized changes to one's web site. For businesses selling information-related products over the Internet, such as software vendors that may allow their paying customers to download upgrades, there has to be a way to discriminate between paying customers and non-paying individuals.

Security administrators face the risk that an attacker will be able to break into the organization's network. The attacker may be anyone with motivation to obtain access. The attacks may range from direct attacks by both hackers and insiders to automated attacks such as using network worms. Such an attacker might obtain:

- *Read access:* The attacker is able to read or copy confidential information.
- *Write access:* The attacker is able to write to your network. This includes the ability to infect the system with a virus or plant Trojan horses or back-doors. The attacker may also destroy confidential information by deleting it or writing over it.
- *Denial of service:* The purpose of some attacks is simply to deny authorized users of normal network services. An attack may be launched which consumes CPU time, network bandwidth, or fills up memory.

Security risks in using a server on the Internet include inappropriate configuration of ftp (file transfer protocol) settings. If ftp access is allowed to your server, it is essential to properly configure it to prevent unauthorized modifications to files.

There must be a secure communication link of data transmission between interconnected host computer systems of the network. A major form of communication security on the network is cryptography to safeguard transmitted data confidentiality. Cryptographic algorithms may be either symmetric (private key) or asymmetric (public key). The two popular encryption methods are link-level security and end-to-end security. The former safeguards traffic independently on every communication link while the latter safeguards messages from the source to the ultimate destination. Link-level enciphers the communications line at the bit level; data is deciphered upon entering the nodes. End-to-end enciphers information at the entry point to the network and deciphers information at the exit point. Unlike link-level, security exists over information inside the nodes.

There should be a general or a specific list of authorized users. Questions to be answered are:

▶ Who is allowed into the facilities?
▶ When may they enter?
▶ What is the purpose of the visit?

A variety of tools are available to help the security manager implement the security plan.

These include:
▶ Encryption tools
▶ Route and packet filtering
▶ Firewalls

Each company should have a network security policy. Each company should also have an internal corporate security policy. An organization must decide how critical it is to protect the integrity of its computing system and how critical is the security of its web site.

The internal security plan should be distributed to everyone who uses the facilities. Employees should be given written guidance upon the proper use of passwords. They should be informed about the types of words that should not be used as passwords. There should be a policy concerning how frequently the password is to be changed.

There must be positive authentication before a user can have access to the on-line application, network environment, nature of applications, terminal identification, and so on. Information should be provided on "a need to know" basis only.

Access controls should exist to use a specific terminal or application. Date and time constraints along with file usage may be enumerated. Unauthorized use may deactivate or lock a terminal. Diskless workstations may result in a safer network environment.

Passwords

Most local area network or communication software packages contain encryption and security features. Passwords are included in virtually every package. However, passwords often do not provide adequate protection. People generally don't select good passwords or change them frequently enough. From a security perspective it is often not too difficult for hackers to breach security by guessing passwords.

Each company should have a password policy. The effectiveness of passwords is greatly diminished because users do not select good passwords. Many hackers are able to guess passwords because people tend to make certain mistakes. Passwords should never be shared with other individuals. Passwords should not be written down. Passwords should be easy to remember. If one needs to write down the password to remember it, the purpose of the password is defeated. Users should be given certain guidelines:

▷ Users should not select a password that is a word in English or any language. Hackers often use dictionaries to guess passwords. Passwords should not consist of words or names found in encyclopedias.

▷ Users should avoid patterns like *123456*, *12468*, *asdf* or *qwerty*, from the keyboard.

▷ Geographical names, such as Vegas or Florida, should not be used.

▷ Many computer systems require the password contain numerals in addition to alphabetic characters. Many people then use a word, appended by a single number, usually one (e.g., CAT1 or 1CAT). Hackers are easily able to overcome this. They know that most people will select a word and append it with the numeral one.

▷ Users should be encouraged to use a combination of upper and lower case characters. Non-alphabetic characters can also make it more difficult for hackers to guess passwords.

▷ An excellent technique to create a password is to use the first letter of a phrase to create a password. For example, the phrase, "*I Was Born In New York*" would yield the password "*IWBINY.*" This is not a word that is easily guessed. It is also easy for the user to remember.

▷ Users should be required to change their passwords at periodic intervals. This can be accomplished by programming the computer system to require the users to provide new passwords. The system should check to ensure that users do not use the same password again, or select a password that they have used over the last few months. A history should be kept of older passwords to prevent the users from using the same passwords again.

All users should be provided with security guidelines. It is very beneficial to give new users a small course in taking security precautions and selecting a good password. Users must be motivated and they must understand why selecting a good password is essential. The following web site provides users with information about selecting a good password. It also helps users evaluate the strength of their existing password(s): www.symantec.com/security_response/index.jsp

Passwords provide good protection from casual or amateur hackers. Professional or experienced hackers are typically able to bypass the password system. The UNIX environment is quite common and is frequently used. Software programs are available that can assist new hackers, even those with limited knowledge, to find or guess passwords. The aim of most hackers is to obtain unlimited access to the computer system. This is typically accomplished by:

- finding bugs or errors in the system software
- taking advantage of an incorrect installation
- looking for human errors

Many hackers are authorized users, with limited access to the system, trying to get unlimited access. These hackers will have a valid user id and password, and will look for weaknesses in the system that may be exploited.

In most UNIX systems, passwords are stored in an encrypted file. Some systems use a shadow password file where the original data is stored. Passwords are generally encrypted using the Data Encryption Standard (DES) algorithm. A key is used to encrypt and decrypt passwords.

The type of encryption method used is essentially irreversible. While it is easy to encrypt a password, it is extremely difficult, almost impossible, to decrypt it. It is nonetheless possible for hackers to discover the passwords through brute force. If a password consists of only six lowercase characters, a hacker can find the password rather quickly. It is, therefore, critical that passwords for accounts that are likely to attract hackers not consist of simply lowercase characters.

A serious design flaw can sometimes result in the creation of a "universal password." Such a password satisfies the requirements of the login program without the hacker actually knowing the true and correct password. In one case, for example, a hacker could enter an overly long password. The overly long password would end up overwriting the actual password, thus allowing the hacker unauthorized access.

Modem connections

Any time a user is able to connect to the network using a modem, additional risks are introduced into the system. Certain precautions can be taken to minimize risks associated with dial-in modems.

It is important to realize that simply keeping the telephone number secret is not sufficient. Many hackers dial the entire prefix of telephone numbers and they could randomly discover your telephone number.

In the past, many companies used dial-back techniques to reduce the dial in modem risk. Nowadays, with caller-id, the same objective may be accomplished.

Essentially, the network will allow users access only from certain pre-identified telephone numbers. The obvious disadvantage of this technique is that the telephone numbers of authorized users must be arranged in advance. This makes it especially difficult for users who travel.

Another way to minimize risk of dial-in modems is to use hardware encryption devices on both ends of the connection. These devices, however, tend to be expensive.

A good telecommunications software program will have numerous protocol options, enabling communications with different types of equipment. Some communications programs do error checking of information or software programs received. Desirable features in telecommunications programs include menus providing help, telephone directory storage, and automatic log-on and redial.

Saboteur's Tools

While in recent years ingenious procedures have been developed to preserve computer security, many computer systems are still astonishingly insecure. Saboteurs may use a wide variety of tools and techniques to overcome security. Some of the methods are as follows:

Trojan Horse: The saboteur places a hidden program within the normal programs of the business. The computer continues to function normally, while the hidden program is free to collect data, make secret modifications to programs and files, erase or destroy data, and even cause a complete shutdown of operations. Trojan horses can be programmed to destroy all traces of their existence after execution.

Salami Techniques: The perpetrator can make secret changes to the computer program that cause very small changes that are unlikely to be discovered, but whose cumulative effect can be very substantial. For example, the perpetrator may steal ten cents from the paycheck of each individual and transfer it to his own account.

Back Door or Trap Door: During the development of a computer program, programmers sometimes insert a code to allow them to bypass the standard security procedures. Once the programming is complete, such code may remain in the program either accidentally or intentionally. Attackers rely on their knowledge of this extra code to bypass security.

Time Bomb/Logic Bomb: A code may be inserted into a computer program that causes damage when a predefined condition occurs.

Masquerade: A computer program is written that masquerades or simulates the real program. For example, a program may be written to simulate the log-in screen and related dialogue. When a user attempts to log-in, the program captures the user's ID and password and displays some error message prompting the user to log-in again. The second time, the program allows the user to log-in and the user may never know that the first log-in was fake.

Scavenging: A computer normally does not erase data that is no longer needed. When the user "deletes" some data, that information is not actually destroyed; instead, that space is made available for the computer to write on later. A scavenger may thus be able to steal sensitive data, which the user thought had been deleted, but was actually still available on the computer.

Viruses: Viruses are similar to Trojan horses, except the illegal code is capable of replicating itself. A virus can rapidly spread throughout the system and eradicating it can be expensive and cumbersome. To guard against viruses, there should be care in using programs on diskettes or in copying software from bulletin boards or outside the company. Disks should only be used from verified sources. The best precaution is to use a commercial virus scanner on all downloaded files before using them. An example is McAfee's virus scan. Virus protection and detection is crucial.

Data Manipulation: The most common and easiest way of committing fraud is to add or alter the data before or during input. The best way to detect this type of computer crime is the use of audit software to scrutinize transactions and review audit trails that indicate additions, changes, and deletions were made to data files. The use of batch totals, hash totals, and check digits can also help prevent this type of crime. A batch total is a reconciliation between the total daily transactions processed by the micro and manually determined totals by an individual other than the computer operator. Material deviations must be investigated. A hash total is adding values that would not typically be added together so the total has no meaning other than for control purposes. Examples are employee and product numbers. A check digit is used to ascertain whether an identification number (e.g., account number, employee number) has been correctly entered by adding a calculation to the identification number and comparing the outcome to the check digit.

Piggybacking: Piggybacking is frequently used to gain access to controlled areas. Physical piggybacking occurs when an authorized employee goes through a door using his magnetic ID card, and an unauthorized employee behind him also enters the premises. The unauthorized employee is then in a position to commit a crime. Electronic piggybacking may also occur. For example, an authorized employee leaves his terminal or desktop and an unauthorized individual uses that to gain access.

Phishing: Phishing is the practice of sending fraudulent e-mails requesting confidential information (such as social security number, bank account numbers, and personal identification numbers). These e-mails look official and give you the illusion that they are being sent by a financial institution, government agency, or other legitimate organizations. These e-mails generally include the official logo for the bank or agency and usually reference a potential problem with your account. They often include a link to a Web site or an e-mail address where you are asked to enter or confirm confidential information.

*Spyware:*Spyware is software that is installed onto your computer, usually without your knowledge, to record your online activity for third parties.

Pop-up windows: This is a small window or ad that appears in the window you are viewing. Fraudulent pop-ups may ask for personal information that can be used to access your financial or private information. Often, a pop-up will promise a gift or prize in exchange for personal information after completing a survey or questionnaire.

Considerations in Designing Networks

The architecture of a network includes hardware, software, information link controls, standards, topologies, and protocols. A protocol relates to how computers communicate and transfer information. Security controls must exist over each component within the architecture to assure reliable and correct data exchanges. Otherwise, the integrity of the system may be compromised.

In designing the network, one must consider three factors. First, the user should get the best response time and throughput. Minimizing response time entails shortening delays between transmission and receipt of data; this is especially important for interactive sessions between user applications. Throughput involves transmitting the maximum amount of data per unit of time.

Second, the data should be transmitted along the least-cost path within the network, as long as other factors, such as reliability are not compromised. The least-cost path is generally the shortest channel between devices and involves the use of the fewest number of intermediate components. Furthermore, low priority data can be transmitted over relatively inexpensive telephone lines, while high priority data can be transmitted over expensive high-speed satellite channels.

Third, maximum reliability should be provided to assure proper receipt of all data traffic. Network reliability includes not only the ability to deliver error-free data, but also the ability to recover from errors or lost data in the network. The network's diagnostic system should be capable of locating problems with components and perhaps even isolating the component from the network.

Network Media

The considerations in selecting a network medium are:
- Technical reliability
- Type of business

- Number of individuals who will need to access or update accounting data simultaneously
- Physical layout of existing equipment
- Frequency of updating
- Number of micros
- Compatibility
- Cost
- Geographic dispersion
- Type of network operating software available and support
- Availability of application software
- Expandability in adding additional workstations
- Restriction to PCs (or can cheaper terminals be used?)
- Ease of access in sharing equipment and data
- Need to access disparate equipment like other networks and main frames
- Processing needs
- Speed
- Data storage ability
- Maintenance
- Noise
- Connectivity mechanism
- Capability of network to conduct tasks without corrupting data moving through it

Network Topologies

The network configuration or topology is the physical shape of the network in terms of the layout of linking stations. A node refers to a workstation. A bridge is a connection between two similar networks. Network protocols are software implementations providing support for network data transmission. A server is a micro or a peripheral performing tasks such as data storage functions within a local area network (LAN). Network servers are of several types. A dedicated server is a central computer used only to manage network traffic. A computer that is used simultaneously as a local workstation is called a nondedicated server. In general, dedicated servers provide faster network performance since they do not take requests from both local users and network stations. In addition, these machines are not susceptible to crashes caused by local users' errors. Dedicated servers are expensive and cannot be disconnected from the network and used as stand-alone computers. Nondedicated servers have a higher price-performance ratio for companies that need occasional use of the server as a local workstation.

The most common types of network topologies are as follows:

▶ *The hierarchical topology* (also called vertical or tree structure) is one of the most common networks. The hierarchical topology is attractive for several reasons. The software to control the network is simple and the topology provides a concentration point for control and error resolution. However, it also presents potential bottleneck and reliability problems. It is possible that network capabilities may be completely lost in the event of a failure at a higher level.

▶ *The horizontal topology* (or bus topology) is popular in local area networks. Its advantages include simple traffic flow between devices. This topology permits all devices to receive every transmission; in other words, a single station broadcasts to multiple stations. The biggest disadvantage is that since all computers share a single channel, a failure in the communication channel results in the loss of the network. One way to get around this problem is through the use of redundant channels. Another disadvantage with this topology is that the absence of concentration points makes problem resolution difficult. Therefore, it is more difficult to isolate faults to any particular component. A bus network usually needs a minimum distance between taps to reduce noise. Identifying a problem requires the checking of each system element. A bus topology is suggested for shared databases but is not good for single-message switching. It employs minimum topology to fill a geographic area, while at the same time having complete connectivity.

▶ *The star topology* is a very popular configuration and it is widely used for data communication systems. The software for star topology is not complex and controlling traffic is simple. All traffic emanates from the hub or the center of the star. In a way, the star configuration is similar to the hierarchical network; however, the star topology has more limited distributed processing capabilities. The hub is responsible for routing data traffic to other components. It is also responsible for isolating faults, which is a relatively simple matter in the star configuration. The star network, like the hierarchical network, is subject to potential bottleneck at the hub and may cause serious reliability problems. One way to minimize this problem and enhance reliability is by establishing a redundant back-up of the hub node. A star network is best when there is a need to enter and process data at many locations with day-end distribution to different remote users. Here, information for general use is sent to the host computer for subsequent processing. It is easy to identify errors in the system, since each communication must go through the central controller. Maintenance is easily performed if the central computer fails the network. There is a high initial cost in setting up the system because each node requires hookup to the host computer in addition to the mainframe's cost. Expansion is easy, as all that is needed is to run a wire from the terminal to the host computer.

▶ *The ring topology* is another popular approach to structuring a network. The data in a ring network flows in a circular direction, usually in one direction only. The data flows from one station to the next station; each station receives the data and then transmits it to the next station. One main advantage of the ring network is that bottlenecks, such as those found in the hierarchical or star networks, are relatively uncommon. There is an organized structure. The primary disadvantage of the ring network is that a single channel ties all of the components in a network. The entire network can be lost if the channel between two nodes fails. Establishing a backup channel can usually alleviate this problem. Other ways to overcome this problem is by using switches to automatically route the traffic around the failed node, or install redundant cables. A ring network is more reliable and less expensive when there is a minimum level of communication between micros. This type of network is best when there are several users at different locations who have to access updated data on a continual basis. Here, more than one data transmission can occur simultaneously. The system is kept current on an ongoing basis. The ring network permits accountants within the firm to create and update shared databases. With a ring, there is greater likelihood of error incidence compared to a star because numerous intervening parties handle data. In light of this, the accountant should recommend that data in a ring system make an entire circle before being removed from the network.

▶ The mesh topology provides a very reliable, though complex, network. Its structure makes it relatively immune to bottlenecks and other failures. The multiplicity of paths makes it relatively easy to route traffic around failed components or busy nodes.

LANs and WANs

The major differences in WANs and LANs means that their topologies usually take on different shapes. A WAN structure tends to be more irregular. Since an organization generally leases the lines at a considerable cost, an attempt is usually made to keep the lines fully utilized. To accomplish this, data is often routed for a geographical area through one channel; hence, the irregular shape of the WAN network.

The LAN topology tends to be more structured. Since the channels in a LAN network are relatively inexpensive, the owners of a LAN are generally not concerned with the maximum utilization of channels. Furthermore, since LANs usually reside in a building or a plant, such networks tend to be inherently more structured and ordered. LANs are flexible, fast, and compatible. They maximize equipment utilization, reduce processing cost, reduce errors, and provide ease of information flow. LANs use ordinary telephone lines, coaxial cables, fiber optics, and other devices like interfaces. Fiber optics results in good performance and reliability but are of high cost. LAN performance depends on physical design, protocols supported, and transmission bandwidth. Bandwidth is the frequency range of a channel and reflects transmission speed along the network. As more devices become part of the LAN, transmission speed decreases.

Two or more LANs may be interconnected. Each node becomes a cluster of stations (subnetworks). The LANs communicate with each other.

Advantages of interfacing networks include:

▶ Total network costs are lower.
▶ There is flexibility in having individual subnetworks meet particular needs.
▶ More reliable and higher cost subnetworks can be used for critical activities and vice versa.
▶ If one LAN fails, the other LAN still functions.
▶ Disadvantages of interfacing networks include:
▶ Complexity is greater.
▶ Some network functions may not be able to go across network boundaries.

Communications Security

Communication systems are used to link data between two or more sites. The communication system should be reliable, private and secure. Communication systems are frequently affected by environmental factors, hardware malfunction and software problems.

Attacks on computers that do not require physical access fall under the domain of communications security. The increased use of computer technology has also increased dependence on telecommunications. All types of data, including sound, video, and traditional data, are transferred between computers over networks. Communications security means ensuring that the physical links between the computer networks function at all times. This also means that during data transmission, breakdowns, delays, and disturbances are prevented. Care must be taken to prevent unauthorized individuals from tapping, modifying, or otherwise intercepting data transmission. Six considerations in communications security are:

Line Security: Line security is concerned with restricting unauthorized access to the communication lines connecting the various parts of the computer systems.

Transmission Security: Transmission security is concerned with preventing unauthorized interception of communication.

Digital Signature: This is used to authenticate the sender or message integrity to the receiver. A secure digital signature process is comprised of (1) a method of signing a document making forgery infeasible and (2) validating that the signature is the one of whom it purports to be.

Cryptographic Security: Cryptography is the science of secret writing. The purpose of cryptographic security is to render the information unintelligible if transmission is intercepted by unauthorized individuals. When the information is to be used, it can be decoded. Security coding (encryption) of sensitive data is necessary. A common method is the Data Encryption Standard (DES). For even greater security, double encryption may be used in which encryption is processed twice using two different keys. (One may also encrypt files on a hard disk to prevent an intruder from reading the data). Encryption of data is a security procedure in which a program encodes data prior to transmission and another program decodes the data after transmission. Encoding is important when confidential data that can be electronically monitored are transmitted between geographically separated locations.

Emission Security: Electronic devices emit electromagnetic radiation which can be intercepted, without wires, by unauthorized individuals. Emission security is concerned with preventing the emission of such radiation.

Technical Security: Technical security is concerned with preventing the use of devices such as a microphone, transmitters, or wiretaps to intercept data transmission. Security modems may be used allowing only authorized users to access confidential data. A modem may have graduated levels of security. Different users may be assigned different security codes. There can be password and call back features. There may be built-in audit trail capabilities allowing you to monitor who is accessing private files.

Many companies are using Value Added Networks (VANs). VANs offer both communication services as well as specialized data processing. It is important to consider the security provided by VANs. Generally, a company has no direct control over a VANs' security. However, VANs' security has a direct effect on the client organization's overall security.

Communication security may be in the form of:

▶ *Access control:* Guards against improper use of the network. For example, KERBEROS is commercial authentication software that is added to an existing security system to verify a user's existence to assure he or she is not an impostor. KERBEROS does this by encrypting passwords transmitted around networks. Password control and user authentication devices may be used such as Security Dynamics' SecurID (800-SECURID) and Vasco Data Security's Access Key II (800-238-2726). Do not accept a prepaid call if it is not from a network user. Hackers do not typically spend their own funds. Review data communications billings and verify each host-to-host connection. Review all dial-up terminal users. Are the telephone numbers unlisted and changed periodically? Control specialists should try to make unauthorized access to the network to test whether the security is properly working.

▶ *Identification*: Identifies the origin of a communication within the network such as identifying the entity involved through digital signals or notarization.

▶ *Data confidentiality*: Maintains confidentiality over unauthorized disclosure of information within the communication process.

▶ *Data integrity*: Guards against unauthorized changes (e.g., adding, deleting) of data at both the receiving and sending points such as through cryptographic methods. Anti-virus software should be installed at both the network server and workstations. Detection programs are available to alert users when viruses enter the system.

▶ *Authentication*: Substantiates the identity of an originating or user entity within the network. There is verification that the entity is actually the one being claimed and that the information being transmitted is appropriate. Examples of security controls are passwords, time stamping, synchronized checks, nonrepudiation, and multiple-way handshakes. Biometric authentication methods measure body characteristics with the use of equipment attached to the workstation. Retinal laser beams may also be used. Keystroke dynamics is another possibility for identification.

▶ *Digital signature*: Messages are signed with a private key.

▶ *Routing control*: Inhibits data flow to insecure network elements such as identified unsecure relays, links, or subnetworks.

▶ *Traffic padding*: A traffic analysis of data for reasonableness.

▶ *Interference minimization*: Radar/radio transmission interference must be eliminated or curtailed. There are various ways to backup data in networks. For a small network, one workstation may be used as the backup and restore for other nodes. In a large network, several servers may perform backups since the failure of one could have disastrous effects on the entire system. Access to backup files must be strictly controlled.

Token-Ring and Ethernet Networks

Traditional Token-Ring and Ethernet networks work on the broadcast principle. These networks send information in units called frames. Each frame contains information about a variety of items, including the sender's and the receiver's address. The sender broadcasts a frame that every receiver can see. At any given moment only one computer in the network is broadcasting and all other computers act as receivers. Another computer may broadcast after the first computer's broadcast is completed. While all machines on a network can see the broadcasting computer's frame, under ideal conditions, only the computer whose address matches the receiver's address in the frame should be able to access the frame's contents.

Sniffers

Sniffers are programs designed to capture certain information. Network managers frequently use sniffers to analyze network traffic and network statistics. Hackers, however, may use sniffers to steal information, such as passwords. Taking certain actions can minimize sniffing risk. The most obvious solution is to limit access. If the hacker is unable to access the LAN, sniffers cannot be used. However, it is often possible to restrict access to networks too tightly; hence, other alternatives need to be considered. Switched versions of token-ring and Ethernet networks may be used to minimize sniffing. With a switched LAN, each user has his own port on the switch. A virtual connection is established with the destination port for each frame sent. If destination address in the frame does not match, the risk associated with sniffing is significantly reduced. Switched networks tend to be more expensive. Moreover, it is rare to find completely switched networks.

Probably the best way to minimize sniffing risk is to use data encryption. In such a system, it is important that the key is never sent over the network. Traditional information, such as the time, is used to enhance the encryption scheme.

Data Flow

Data switching equipment is used to route data through the network to its final destinations. For instance, data switching equipment is used to route data around failed or busy devices or channels.

Routers at each site are used to communicate with routers at other sites. Routers provide information about the individuals and the resources available in the LAN. Routers are responsible for directing the flow of information. It is possible to configure the routers so that certain types of routers, such as ftp or telnet do not allow either incoming or outgoing access. It is also possible to enable or disable certain routers to receive information from only certain network addresses. Route and packet filtering requires significant technical knowledge as well as time. Most routers do not provide a security or audit trail. You need to know:

▶ Who tried to break in to the computer system?
▶ How frequently they tried?
▶ What means and methods were used to attempt the break-in?

142

Data Transmission

Data transmission between computers in a network uses one of three methods.

▷ Simplex transmission is in one direction only. An example of simplex transmission is radio or television transmission. Simplex transmission is rare in computer networks due to the one-way nature of data transmission.

▷ Half-duplex transmission is found in many systems. In a half-duplex system, information can flow in both directions. However, it is not possible for the information to flow in both directions simultaneously. In other words, once a query is transmitted from one device, it must wait for a response to come back.

▷ A full-duplex system can transmit information in both directions simultaneously; it does not have the intervening stop-and-wait aspect of half-duplex systems. For high throughput and fast response time, full-duplex transmission is frequently used in computer applications.

Security Layers

Security should be provided in different layers. Security must exist over networking facilities and telecommunication elements. Controls must be placed over both host computers and subnetworks.

Network traffic may be over many subnetworks, each having their own security levels depending on confidentiality and importance. Therefore, different security services and controls may be required. Security aspects of each subnetwork have to be distributed to the gateways so as to incorporate security and controls in routing decisions.

Network Backup

Backup capability is an especially important feature of networks. For instance, if one computer fails, another computer in the network can take over the load. This might be critical in certain industries such as financial institutions.

Secure Sockets Layer

When *Secure Sockets Layer* (SSL) is enabled, a web browser will display a lock or another symbol to indicate that the data transfer is secure. Another way to tell that the web site is secure is by looking at its address: the web site address should start with "https://" rather than simply "http://." Most web-based monetary transactions are secured using SSL. Many web server/client products support SSL connections. To transact on the web, one needs access to such a server as well as a digital certificate.

While using SSL for encryption greatly enhances security and confidentiality, it does slow the communication interchange. All the data has to be encrypted and then decrypted.

Secure Sockets Layer protocol was developed by Netscape. SSL operates by layering a security protocol on top of an underlying connection transport protocol such as HTTP, Telnet, NNTP, FTP and TCP/IP. SSL is built in to Netscape's client and server products. When building a web site, one can enable SSL by configuring a security-enabled http (https) process on the server. Web pages that require SSL access can be specified. Common Gateway Interface (CGI) routines can be written on the server side to integrate SSL into existing applications.

SSL provides data encryption and checks for data integrity. It provides server authentication, and if required, client authentication, for a TCP/IP connection. SSL is an open and nonproprietary protocol. Encryption, decryption and authentication are performed transparently for applications utilizing the SSL protocol.

SSL is used extensively to encrypt and authenticate communications on the World Wide Web (WWW) between clients and servers. The *Transport Layer Security* (TLS) standard by the Internet Engineering Task Force (IETF) is based on SSL.

A user can confirm and authenticate a SSL server's identity. Such confirmation is necessary when the user is sending sensitive information, such as a credit card number, to the server and wants to check the server's identity. The digital certificate serves as the key to SSL. It is used to prove authenticity. Certificate Authorities (CA) such as VeriSign Inc. issue digital certificates. Anyone with the correct software can become a certificate authority, but there are only certain trusted CA's that a web browser will accept. It is possible to tell the web browser which CA it should accept.

Public-key cryptography techniques may be used to check if a server's certificate and public ID are valid and were issued by a trusted CA. Similarly, a server can confirm a user's identity by checking that the client's certificate and public ID are valid and were issued by a trusted CA.

Public key cryptography greatly facilitates key management. Without public key cryptography, encrypted communication could take place between two or more users only if they shared the keys. The users need to maintain a secure connection to share the secret key. This means that each user would have to maintain several keys for communicating with various users.

Public key cryptography allows parties to communicate securely without sharing secret keys. Each party establishes a key pair: one private key and one public key. The public key is published and is available to all nodes on a network. The public key is used to encrypt messages to the node. The private key is used to decrypt the messages. It never leaves its node on the network.

Public key cryptography is used to create digital signatures and sign documents. The document is signed using the private key, but other users can verify the signature using the public key. The digital certificate consists of the name and other information about the user along with the user's public key. A trusted certificate authority signs the information on the digital certificate and verifies the identity of a user. The following steps are typically taken:

- A user creates a public/private key pair.
- The private key is stored with the user.
- The public key is given to a trusted authority.
- The trusted authority creates a digital signature for the user and provides a digital certificate.
- The digital certificate may be published or attached to messages being digitally signed by the user.
- Other users may verify the signature and authenticate the user's identity using the digital certificate.

The *Transmission Control Protocol/Internet Protocol* (TCP/IP) provides the rules for transporting and routing data over the Internet. Protocols such as the HyperText Transport Protocol (HTTP) use the TCP/IP to carry out tasks such as displaying web pages. The SSL protocol runs in the middle between TCP/IP and other higher level protocols, such as HTTP. It runs above TCP/IP, but below the higher level protocols. SSL utilizes TCP/IP on behalf of the higher level protocols. This allows SSL enabled clients and servers to authenticate themselves and makes an encrypted connection possible.

Confidentiality in a SSL connection is ensured through encryption. All information transported between the client and server is encrypted in a SSL connection. The sending software encrypts and the receiving software decrypts the data. SSL connection also provides assurance that the data has not been tampered with or altered in transit.

The "strength" of an SSL connection depends on the bit level. For example, 40-bit SSL connections tend to be rather weak, whereas a 128-bit SSL connection is extremely strong. 128-bits is approximately three hundred and forty septillion times (340,000,000 ,000,000,000,000,000,000) larger than 40-bits.

128-bit encryption is only available for American and Canadian residents. It is presently illegal for US companies to export internationally anything above a 56-bit encryption. Software security companies are trying to overcome these export restrictions by developing encryption technology outside of the United States.

The SSL protocol includes two sub-protocols. The *SSL Record Protocol* defines the format that will be used for data transmission. The *SSL Handshake Protocol* determines how the record protocol will exchange data between a SSL server and a SSL client when the SSL connection is first established. It is used to either authenticate the server to the client, or the client to the server. It also allows the client and server to select from the various cryptographic algorithms or ciphers supported by both the client and the server.

Both public-key and symmetric key encryption is used by the SSL protocol. While symmetric key encryption tends to be faster, public-key encryption provides better authentication. Commonly used ciphers include:

- Data Encryption Standard (DES) is a commonly used encryption algorithm. Triple DES applies DES three times and supports 168-bit encryption. Its key size makes it one of the strongest ciphers supported by SSL.
- Digital Signature Algorithm (DSA) is used for authentication of digital signatures.
- Key Exchange Algorithm (KEA) is used for key exchange.
- Message Digest (MD5) algorithm.
- RSA is a public-key algorithm used for authentication and encryption. RSA key exchange algorithm is used for SSL connections. It is one of the most frequently used ciphers.
- Secure Hash Algorithm (SHA-1).
- SKIPJACK. A classified symmetric-key algorithm used in FORTEZZA compliant hardware. The FORTEZZA encryption system is used by the U.S. government agencies for sensitive but unclassified data. FORTEZZA ciphers use the Key Exchange Algorithm (KEA) for SSL instead of the RSA key-exchange algorithm. FORTEZZA cards and DSA are used for client authentication.

The RSA public-key cryptography system is most prevalent in commercial applications. It provides encryption, decryption, digital signatures and authentication capabilities. Performance can suffer when using public key cryptography. Therefore, public key encryption is typically limited to digital signatures or encrypting a small amount of data. Symmetric key encryption, such as DES and RC2 and RC4, is typically used for encrypting bulk data.

The supported ciphers for both the client and the server can easily be enabled or disabled. During the handshake, the client and server determine the strongest common enabled cipher suite and it is used for the SSL connection.

Security administrators should decide which cipher suites to enable or disable. Administrators should consider the nature of the data, the need for confidentiality and security, and the speed of the cipher. The national origin of the parties is another consideration since certain ciphers may only be used within the USA and Canada. Thus, if an organization disables the weaker ciphers, it automatically restricts access to clients within the United States and Canada; an international client may access the server only if it has a special Global Server ID.

SSL Handshake

The following sequence of events typically takes place in an SSL connection:

- The client provides the server with the client's SSL version number, cipher settings, and a variety of other communications related data.

▶ The server provides the client with the server's SSL version number, cipher settings, and a variety of other communications related data.

▶ The server certificate is sent. If necessary, the client's certificate is requested.

▶ The client authenticates the server. If there is an error and the server cannot be authenticated, the client is warned that an encrypted and authenticated connection cannot be established.

▶ The client creates a "pre-master" secret for the SSL connection and encrypts it with the server's public key. The encrypted pre-master is then sent to the server. The client may also sign and send data as well as its certificate to authenticate itself, if requested by the server.

▶ The session will be terminated if the server cannot authenticate the client.

▶ The server uses its private key to decrypt the pre-master secret and to generate the "master" secret. The client generates the master secret using the same pre-master secret.

▶ Using the master secret, session keys are generated by both the client and the server. The session keys are symmetric and are used to encrypt and decrypt data. The keys are used to ensure that the data is not tampered with between the time that it is sent and the time that it is received, and that data integrity has not been compromised.

▶ The SSL session begins once the SSL handshake is completed. Both the client and the server use the session keys to encrypt and decrypt data and to verify the data integrity.

Authentication

Both client and server authentication requires encrypting data with one key of a public-private key pair and decrypting it with the other key. For server authentication, the client encrypts the pre-master secret with the server's public key. The associated private key alone can decrypt the pre-master secret. This provides the client with reasonable assurance about the server's identity.

For client authentication, the client encrypts some random pieces of data using the client's private key. In other words, it creates a digital signature that can be validated using the public key in the client's certificate, only if the corresponding private key had been used. If the server cannot validate the digital signature, authentication fails and the session will be terminated.

SSLRef

SSLRef is an advanced software developer's tool-kit. Its purpose is to help developers provide security features in TCP/IP applications using the SSL protocol. ANSI C source code is provided for incorporation into TCP/IP applications. SSLRef may be downloaded for free for noncommercial use. While there are no license restrictions, there are export restrictions on SSLRef.

Kerberos

Kerberos is a network authentication protocol that uses secret-key cryptography. Kerberos protocol is used in a client/server environment to authenticate the client to the server and the server to the client. After authenticating client/server identity, Kerberos may be used to encrypt data. Kerberos does not send across any data that may allow an attacker to learn secret information and impersonate the user.

Kerberos is available for free in the form of source code from the Massachusetts Institute of Technology. It is also available in commercial software products from several vendors.

When a client accesses a network service, the client asserts to the server that it is running on behalf of an authorized user. Without authentication, there is virtually no security. With Kerberos authentication, the client proves its identity to the server.

In the traditional environment, a user's identity is verified or authenticated by checking the user's password during the login process. Password based authentication has several drawbacks in the networked environment. The most critical problem is that hackers can intercept passwords sent across the network.

Without Kerberos authentication, the user would need to enter a password to access *each* network service. This is, at a minimum, inconvenient. Moreover, it still does not provide security when accessing services on a remote machine. Without encryption, it would be easy for anyone to intercept the password during transit. Kerberos eliminates the need to use passwords. Instead, a key is used to encrypt and decrypt short messages and provide the basis for authentication.

Kerberos uses a series of encrypted messages to prove that a client is running on behalf of a particular user. The client, to prove its identity, presents a ticket issued by the Kerberos Authentication Server. Secret information, such as a password, that only an authorized user would know, is contained in the ticket.

Kerberos is not effective against password guessing attacks. It is, therefore, essential for the user to select a good password. Otherwise, it may be possible for a hacker who intercepts a few encrypted messages to launch an attack by randomly trying passwords to see if the messages decrypt correctly. If a hacker is able to guess the password, he will be able to impersonate the user.

Kerberos assumes that the workstations or machines are reasonably secure and only the network connections are vulnerable to attack. A trusted path for passwords is required. For example, if the password is entered into a program containing a Trojan horse (i.e., the program has been modified to capture certain information), Kerberos will not provide any protection. Moreover, if transmissions across the path between the user and the authentication program can be intercepted, Kerberos will be ineffective.

Both the user and the network service must have keys registered with the Kerberos Authentication Server. The user's key is derived from a user-selected password. The network service key is selected randomly.

A version of Kerberos called Bones is available for international users. The Bones version was created since the United States restricts export of cryptography. All the DES routines have been stripped from Bones. Many types of software used by the international community require Kerberos. Bones is used as a substitute to "trick" other software into believing that Kerberos is installed. International users can get Encrypted Bones or E-Bones, which does provide encryption.

To use Kerberos, a Kerberos principal must be established. A Kerberos principal is like a regular account on a machine. Certain information, such as the user name and password, are associated with each principal. The information is encrypted and stored in the Kerberos database. Kerberos is essentially transparent from the user's perspective. To be effective, Kerberos has to be integrated into the computer system. Kerberos protects only data from software that is configured to use Kerberos.

The Kerberos Authentication Server maintains a database of passwords or encryption keys. It is, therefore, critical to protect the server system. The server, if possible, should be physically secure. Ideally, the machine should be dedicated to running the authentication server. Access to the machine should be strictly restricted.

While Kerberos is freely available from MIT, it is not officially supported. Several companies have taken reference implementations from MIT and provide commercially supported products.

Each user's initial password has to be registered with the authentication server. The registration procedure depends upon the number of users. In person registration provides the best control if the number of users is small. Other procedures, such as using a login program on a trusted system, may be used when the number of users is large.

Several tools can enhance the security provided by Kerberos. One-time passwords generated by a device are particularly useful. Kerberos cannot protect against a hacker guessing or stealing user passwords. One-time passwords eliminate that problem. Commercial products are available that combine one-time passwords with Kerberos.

Internet Sources for Information about Kerberos

Additional information about Kerberos is available from http://web.mit.edu/kerberos/www.

Vendors for Kerberos

The web sites for some vendors that sell or support Kerberos are as follows:
- www.cybersafe.ltd.uk
- www.latticesoft.com

149

▶ www.stonecast.net
▶ www.wrq.com

Firewalls

Firewalls are frequently used to overcome some of the problems associated with route and packet filtering. The firewall is a buffer between an organization's internal network and the external world. It is possible to configure the network such that outgoing data may travel freely across the firewall but incoming data is restricted. It is also possible to configure it so that only email may go in and out the computer and no other type of communication is allowed to take place.

The purpose of a firewall is to allow authorized traffic and restrict unauthorized traffic. A firewall is used to control access between two networks. A firewall performs two functions:

▶ restricts or blocks certain traffic
▶ permits certain traffic

Some firewalls are more concerned about restricting unauthorized traffic while others place greater emphasis on permitting traffic. Senior management in an organization should play an integral part in determining the kind of access to permit or deny.

A firewall can be very restrictive and allow only email messages to go through. Other firewalls may block certain types of services that are known to cause problems. Most firewalls are configured to protect against unauthenticated interactive logins from external networks. Firewalls can also be configured to allow internal users unrestricted access to outside services, while preventing traffic from the outside to the inside.

Unlike dial-in modem connections, firewalls provide logging and auditing functions for security purposes. For example, security data may be obtained about the number of login attempts and password failures.

Firewalls can't protect against all types of attacks. Many organizations are overly concerned about threats from sources external to the organization. However, firewalls can't protect against internal threats. It is just as easy for internal users to steal propriety data since they don't have to go through the firewall. Other routes to the corporate network, as well as threats from internal users should be considered, and firewalls should be one part of the organization's security plan.

While several firewall vendors are offering virus protection tools, firewalls are not very effective against protection from viruses. It is relatively easy to transfer virus files over the network and relatively difficult to protect and search for such viruses. A file could be mailed to an internal host, copied and executed, and in general, firewalls cannot protect against such attacks.

A virus can come from many sources, not only via transfers from the Internet. Virus protection should be a part of an organization's overall security plan. Steps should be taken to protect against viruses from all sources, and especially internal sources where floppy disks are exchanged. Virus scanning software should be installed on each machine and should run automatically when the machine is booted.

Firewall policies should consider the nature of the data to be protected. If the data require a very high level of security, the organization must assess whether the data should even be accessible via the Internet. With top secret data, it may be wise to isolate it from the main corporate network.

The firewall system that limits access to a computer network by routing users to replicated Web pages is a proxy server. A proxy server maintains copies of web pages to be accessed by specified users. Outsiders are directed there, and more important information is not available from this access point.

Setting up a Firewall

The cost of setting up a firewall can range from virtually free to several thousands, even hundreds of thousands of dollars. When selecting a firewall system, one should consider not only the initial setup cost, but also the cost of ongoing maintenance and support.

The organization must decide the level of access that will be granted through the firewall.

At one end, the firewall may be set up to block all services except those that are absolutely essential to establish connection. At the other end, the firewall may simply be used for monitoring and audit purposes. Most organizations would not want to be at either extreme. The sensitivity of the data will determine an organization's stance. The organization should explicitly decide what services should be permitted, denied, or simply monitored.

There are two basic types of firewalls. *Network* level firewalls rely on the source/destination addresses and ports in individual IP packets. Network level firewalls generally route traffic directly and require an assigned IP address. Network level firewalls are typically fast and transparent to users.

Application level firewalls typically act as hosts running proxy servers. A proxy server or an application gateway mediates traffic between a protected network and the Internet. Proxy servers are frequently used to prevent traffic from passing directly through networks. Greater logging or support for user authentication is provided.

Application level firewalls do not allow any traffic directly between the networks. They control access as well as log and audit traffic passing through them. While improvements have been made, the performance of application level firewalls may not be as good and they may not be as transparent to the user as network level firewalls.

Future firewalls will contain the characteristics of both network level firewalls and application level firewalls. Network level firewalls will keep better track of information that goes through them, and application level firewalls will become more transparent. The overall effect will be better performance with elaborate logging and auditing functions. Encryption of data passing through the firewall is becoming increasingly common. With encryption, an organization can have multiple points of connectivity with the Internet and not be as concerned about password or data sniffing programs.

Resources for Firewalls

Resources required to protect a site using a firewall are likely to vary considerably due to variations in traffic type and system load. System scalability is important and a faster CPU will not necessarily enhance performance. Sufficient RAM is critical for busy systems to provide adequate performance. A denial-of-service attack can be easily launched against a system with insufficient RAM. At the very least, the system will have a backlog.

Security of DMZ

DMZ or *demilitarized zone* of a firewall refers to the part of the network that does not belong to either the internal network or to the Internet. This is generally the area between the Internet access router and the bastion host. The bastion host is a system that has been fortified against attacks. It is the system on the network where an attack is expected. Bastion hosts may be part of the firewall.

Putting access control lists on the access router creates a DMZ. An access control list contains the rules that define which packets are permitted or denied passage. The access router connects an organization's internal network with the external Internet. An access router is a company's first line of defense against attacks from the Internet. Creating a DMZ allows only authorized services to be accessible by hosts on the Internet. Attackers often try to exploit the relationship between a vulnerable host and other more attractive items.

If a system has several services that mandate different security levels, one option is to divide the DMZ into several separate zones. The effects of a security breach can be minimized by putting together hosts with similar levels of risks. Hence, even if an attacker is able to exploit some bug and gains access, the attacker will be unable to launch an attack against the private network if the bastion hosts are on a separate LAN. This may occur, for example, when the attacker is able to gain access to the web server.

Most organizations do not secure their web servers as strictly and allow services for Internet users that entail certain risks. Unauthenticated users might be able to run CGI or other executable programs on the web server. While this might be reasonable for the web server, it is unacceptable to run such programs on a bastion host, where the entire security mechanism might be compromised.

Services should be split up not only by host but also by networks. The level of trust between hosts on the networks should also be limited.

An organization should use redundant components to achieve maximum security. A single failure, such as a software bug, should not compromise the entire security mechanism. Risk related to software bugs can easily be reduced by:

▶ keeping up-to-date on software fix patches
▶ using products that have been around a while and are well known
▶ running only necessary services

Organizational Policy

The organization must decide which services to permit and which services to deny. This depends, to a great extent, upon the focus of the function of the firewall. An organization may be primarily concerned with allowing access or the organization may be primarily concerned with maintaining security.

If the emphasis is on maintaining security, the organization may decide to block everything and allow access on a limited or case-by-case basis. This way the organization can focus specifically upon the security concerns of the products or services it wishes to permit.

When deciding the services to permit, one should consider:

▶ What effect will allowing this service have on firewall security?
▶ How does permitting the service affect firewall architecture?
▶ Will an attacker be able to exploit an inherent weakness?
▶ How well known is the service?
▶ Is the protocol for this service well known and published?

Restricting Web Access Using Firewalls

An organization may want to restrict web access to prevent users from viewing sites not related to their work. An organization may also want to block access to sites it deems inappropriate. While firewalls may be used to block access, it is a difficult task.

It is relatively easy for individuals to find an alternate route to a blocked site. Site-blocking products are typically not effective and are easy to circumvent. For example, inappropriate web pages may be fetched through email. It is virtually impossible to block everything.

Denial of Service Attacks

Attackers sometime decide to launch denial of service attacks by crashing, flooding or disrupting the network or firewall. Due to the distributed nature of networks, it is virtually impossible to prevent such attacks. For time-critical jobs on the Internet, it is essential to have a contingency plan in case the network is attacked or its capability degraded.

Using FTP, Telnet, Archie, Gophers through Firewalls

FTP (File Transfer Protocol) is usually supported in firewalls by using either a proxy server or allowing connections to networks at a restricted port range. Sometime, FTP can be achieved by allowing the users to download files via the Web. Telnet is generally supported using an application proxy. Configuring a router to permit outbound connections using screening rules can also support Telnet. Both Gopher and Archie can be supported through Web proxies.

Pretty Good Privacy (PGP)

Pretty Good Privacy (PGP) can be used to encrypt email messages or digitally sign messages. Encrypting messages provides the user with privacy. If the encrypted email is intercepted, it will appear to be garbage to the unauthorized recipient. Digital signatures can be used when the content of the message is not secret, but the sender wants to authenticate his identity and confirm that he wrote the message. PGP has proven itself to be very effective at protecting electronic messages.

PGP relies upon a public key encryption scheme. Unlike conventional encryption schemes, with public key encryption, there is no need to have a secure channel over which to share the key. The encryption and decryption keys are different when using such a public key encryption scheme. The public key is used to encrypt the data. It is readily available to the public and is typically available in a public database. The decryption key is private. No one has access to it except the intended recipient.

PGP is available for free for non-commercial use. ViaCrypt PGP is available for commercial use and costs under $100. ViaCrypt PGP is available for commercial use primarily in the United States and Canada. For the international community, commercial versions of PGP are available from Ascom Systec AG.

To use PGP, one must have two key rings: a public one and a private one. The public key ring holds your public key as well as the public keys of people known to you. The private key ring holds the secret or private key or keys.

Public key encryption is much slower compared to conventional. PGP combines two algorithms, namely RSA and IDEA, to encrypt plain text. It is essentially impossible to break the encryption algorithm using brute force. For PGP's IDEA encryption scheme, currently a 128-bit key is required. This means that 2^{128} possible key combinations would be available. Using the fastest current technology it would still take several trillion years to break the encryption scheme.

To launch a successful attack against such a scheme, an attacker must understand the mathematical transformation that takes place between plain text and cipher text. By understanding the mathematical transformation, an attacker might be able to successfully launch an attack. The complexity of the transformation makes it extremely difficult to solve the mathematical problem.

At present, PGP gives you three choices for key size: 512, 768, or 1024 bits. It is also possible to specify the number of bits for your key. As the key size increases, the encryption becomes more secure. The key size affects the program's running time during generation. A 1024-bit key takes approximately 8 times longer to generate than a 384-bit key. This is a one-time process and doesn't need to be repeated unless another key pair is generated. Only the RSA portion is affected by the key size during encryption. The main body of the message is not affected by the key size. Therefore, it is best to use the 1024-bit key size. Some versions of PGP allow key sizes up to 2048-bits. Generating such a key will require a considerable amount of time; it is, however, a one-time process. Individuals running certain versions of PGP may be unable to handle very large keys.

Each time PGP is run, a different session key is generated. This session key is used for IDEA. This enhances the security of PGP.

Using PGP, it is possible to apply a digital signature to a message. If a trusted copy of the sender's public encryption key is available, then it can be used to check the signature on the message. It is impossible for anyone else to create the signature without the secret key. This will also detect if someone has tampered with the message. Digital signature protects the entire message.

If the contents of a message are not secret, but it is essential to allow others to verify the authenticity of the sender, clear signing digital signatures may be used. Clear signing works only on text files, it does not work on binary files.

Key signatures are used to authenticate that the signature really belongs to the sender and not an impostor. If the sender's key is not available, but a trusted source has added his signature to the sender's key, then you may infer that you have a valid copy of the sender's key. A chain of trust may be established for several levels: A trusts B who trusts C, therefore A may trust C. PGP can be configured to specify the number of levels this chain of trust is allowed. One should be cautious when dealing with keys that are several levels removed from your immediate trusted source.

You may sign someone's key if you wish to inform others that you believe the key belongs to that person. Other people may rely on your signature to decide whether or not that person's key is valid.

A key signing party is used to get together various users of PGP. A key signing party's purpose is to sign keys to extend the degree of trust on the web.

If the secret key ring is stolen or lost, the key should be revoked. If a strong pass phrase had been used to encrypt the secret key ring, there is little chance of damage. Both the pass phase and the secret key ring are needed to decrypt a message. Using a backup copy of the secret key ring, a key revocation certificate may be generated and uploaded to one of the public key servers. Before uploading the revocation certificate, it is useful to add a new ID to the old key to inform others what your new key ID will be. Without a backup copy of the secret key ring, it is impossible to create a revocation certificate.

Public key servers are used to make available one's public key. Everyone can use the public database to encrypt messages for you. Although there are several public key servers, it is only necessary to send your key to only one of them. The key server will then send your key to other public key servers.

Security Analysis Tool for Auditing Networks

Security Analysis Tool for Auditing Networks (SATAN) is a tool to help security administrators identify network security problems. SATAN was written by Dan Farmer and Wietse Venema. They explain that they wrote SATAN because computer systems are becoming more dependent on networks, and becoming more vulnerable to attacks via the same networks.

SATAN examines a remote host or set of hosts. It gathers information by remotely probing various services such as *finger*, or *ftp* provided by the host. Potential security flaws and bugs, such as incorrectly setup or configured network services or known system bugs are identified. SATAN's expert system may be used to further investigate potential security problems.

SATAN consists of several programs. Each program tests for a specific potential weakness.

Additional test programs may be added to SATAN by putting their executable file into SATAN's main directory; these programs must have the *.sat* extension. The entire SATAN package, including source code and documentation, is freely available via ftp from various sites.

Courtney

Courtney software is available for free on the Internet. Courtney may be thought of as the anti-SATAN. Courtney monitors attacks from SATAN. Using Courtney, if SATAN probes your system, it notifies you and gives you a chance to trace the probe. Courtney can be downloaded from: www.ciac.org/ciac/bulletins/f-24.shtml.

Vulnerability Testing Using Automated Tools

Security frequently gets compromised because controls are improperly used. Generally, it is not that controls are lacking or that the existing controls are weak, but that the controls are not appropriately configured. Most computer software, for example, comes with default setting. If these settings are left unchanged, security may end up being compromised.

The existence of such controls gives management and users the false impression that their data is secure. They assume that the controls are properly configured and rely upon them. Many hackers exploit well-known security weaknesses. They rely on common errors made by system administrators, such as not configuring the system properly or protecting the system with the latest security patches.

While incompetence or lack of time or other resources certainly contribute to this problem, many administrators may make mistakes because of the nature of the computer systems. Most systems support a wide variety of services and the security mechanism must be flexible enough to meet the needs of a variety of users. The system administrator and users are given the power to enhance or degrade security based upon one's needs. This flexibility can often lead to security weaknesses.

Many automated tools are available to audit the computer system and report potential security weaknesses. Such automated tools can examine thousands of files on a multi-user computer system and identify vulnerabilities that can result from improper use of controls or mismanagement. Such vulnerabilities include poor passwords or failure to update software with security patches. Automated tools may test for adequate virus protection or for the ability to plant Trojan horses or worms.

Such automated tools are available commercially or may be developed in-house to suit an organization's specific needs. These tools typically analyze file content and file attributes to identify vulnerabilities. The automated tools are capable of quickly analyzing and testing thousands of files.

Automated tools for testing security vulnerability are different from automated tools that monitor activity or detect intrusion. Monitors and intrusion detection systems analyze activity as it occurs. Vulnerability testing tools, on the other hand, search for potential weaknesses that may allow an attacker to gain unauthorized access.

Standalone Systems

To identify vulnerabilities in a standalone system, automated testing tools analyze shared executable files. These tools examine a variety of controls such as access controls or controls that are used to configure the system. For example, if the access controls are compromised, a hacker may be able to masquerade as an authorized user. The configuration files and shared executable files may be used to plant a Trojan horse. Vulnerability testing tools are used to analyze files whose modification or disclosure would allow the hacker to circumvent system controls and gain unauthorized access.

Automated vulnerability testing tools may be used to examine the password and access system. The testing tools can check if the passwords are long enough. Short passwords can be guessed easily using brute force. These tools can also check to see if passwords are changed periodically. Passwords should have a limited life and the user should not be allowed to select any password in their password history file. Passwords should be protected and stored in an encrypted file.

To prevent the planting of a Trojan horse program, certain precautions should be taken. User start-up files should be protected from modification. Start-up files are often used to plant Trojan horses because the start-up files are always executed. Write access in a user's personal file space should be limited.

The audit trail should always be maintained. System configuration files and shared binaries must be protected against unauthorized modification. Automated vulnerability testing tools can check to see if modification privileges for system binaries are restricted to systems staff. System binary files should be reviewed for unexpected changes. Only system staff should be able to modify system start-up scripts. Secure defaults should be specified.

In a networked environment, computer systems generally share data and other resources. Security controls for access paths in networks can be reviewed using automated vulnerability testing tools. A network host will not only have the potential vulnerabilities of a stand-alone system, but also the vulnerabilities contained of the networked system. In a networked environment, a hacker could masquerade as an authorized user or another system. Many systems use remote authentication, where the local host relies upon the remote system to authenticate users.

Vulnerability Testing Techniques

Vulnerability tests may audit the system or launch a mock attack. The nature of testing may be passive or active and their scope may be defined as broad or narrow.

Active tests are intrusive and identify vulnerabilities by exploiting them. In contrast, passive tests examine the system to infer the existence of vulnerabilities. An authentication system may be tested using either active testing or passive testing. An active test may launch a dictionary attack or randomly try common or short passwords. If successful, it would log the results for review by security personnel. A passive test of the authentication system might check the protection of a password file. It may copy the password file, encrypt it, and compare encrypted strings. Both types of tests provide useful information. However, active tests are riskier than passive tests. Individual circumstances and professional judgment is required in selecting appropriate tests.

Vulnerability testing programs may be classified according to scope. Their focus may be narrow and they may examine only a single vulnerability or their focus may be broad and they may examine the entire system.

It is possible to use a series of single vulnerability tests to identify risks and vulnerabilities. While single vulnerability tests tend to be simple, they do not generally consider the complete security ramifications. The joint effect of lack of controls may not be revealed through such testing. Weaknesses in multiple controls may compound the effect of the vulnerabilities.

System vulnerability testing provides better information than a series of single vulnerability tests. It is easier to determine the total risk using a system's vulnerability test.

Conclusion

Computer networks play a dominant role in transmitting information within and between firms. A network is simply a set of computers (or terminals) interconnected by transmission paths.

These paths usually take the form of telephone lines; however, other media, such as wireless and infrared transmission, radio waves, and satellites are possible. The network serves one purpose: exchange of data between the computers and/or terminals.

Encryption must be used any time sensitive or confidential information is transmitted. The open nature of the Internet network is such that anything can be read or snatched at many locations between the originating site and the destination site. Encryption should be used not only when transmitting data, but also when putting any secret or sensitive information on the Internet server.

Hackers frequently take advantage of common security holes to break in. For example, they may take advantage of a bug in a software package. It is essential to have the most current version of the software package. The most current version is likely to have the fewest bugs. Most software developers provide patches, which may be downloaded from the developer's web site. These patches frequently fix known security bugs.

Businesses need security for a variety of reasons. The most basic reason is that you don't want accidental or intentional modification of data. In a networked environment, many security problems exist for a business. The more connections that exist, the more complex the system, and the greater the likelihood of security being compromised.

CHAPTER 9

Legal, Ethical, and Tax Issues of Electronic Commerce

Businesses that operate on the Web must comply with the same laws and regulations that govern the operations of all businesses. If they do not, they face the same set of penalties—fines, reparation payments, court-imposed dissolution, and even jail time for officers and owners—that any business faces.

Businesses operating on the Web face two additional complicating factors as they try to comply with the law. First, the Web extends a company's reach beyond traditional boundaries. Thus, a company can become subject to many more laws more quickly than a traditional brick-and-mortar business based in one specific physical location. Second, the Web increases the speed and efficiency of business communications. Further, the Web creates a network of customers who often have significant levels of interaction with each other. Web businesses that violate the law or breach ethical standards can face rapid and intense reactions from many customers and other stakeholders who become aware of the businesses' activities.

Borders and Jurisdiction

Territorial borders in the physical world serve a useful purpose in traditional commerce: They mark the range of culture and reach of applicable laws very clearly. When people travel across international borders, they are made aware of the transition in many ways.

Jurisdiction on the Internet

Governments that want to enforce laws regarding business conduct on the Internet must establish jurisdiction over that conduct. A contract is a promise or set of promises between two or more legal entities - persons or corporations - that provides for an exchange of value (goods, services, or money) between or among them. A tort is an intentional or negligent action taken by a legal entity that causes harm to another legal entity. People or corporations that wish to enforce their rights based on either contract or tort law must file their claims in courts with jurisdiction to hear their cases. A court has sufficient jurisdiction in a matter if it has both subject matter jurisdiction and personal jurisdiction.

Subject-matter Jurisdiction

Subject-matter jurisdiction is a court's authority to decide a particular type of dispute. For example, in the United States, federal courts have subject-matter jurisdiction over issues governed by federal law (such as bankruptcy, copyright, patent, and federal tax matters), and state courts have subject-matter jurisdiction over issues governed by state laws (such as professional licensing and state tax matters). If the parties to a contract are both located in the same state, a state court has subject matter jurisdiction over disputes that arise from the terms of that contract. The rules for determining whether a court has subject-matter jurisdiction are clear and easy to apply. Few disputes arise over subject-matter jurisdiction.

Contracting and Contract Enforcement in Electronic Commerce

Any contract includes three essential elements: an offer, an acceptance, and consideration. The contract is formed when one party accepts the offer of another party. An offer is a commitment with certain terms made to another party, such as a declaration of willingness to buy or sell a product or service. An offer can be revoked as long as no payment, delivery of service, or other consideration has been accepted. An acceptance is the expression of willingness to take an offer, including all of its stated terms. Consideration is the agreed upon exchange of something valuable, such as money, property, or future services. When a party accepts an offer based on the exchange of valuable goods or services, a contract has been created. An implied contract can also be formed by two or more parties that act as if a contract exists, even if no contract has been written and signed.

Use and Protection of Intellectual Property in Online Business

Online businesses must be careful in their use of intellectual property. Intellectual property is a general term that includes all products of the human mind. These products can be tangible or intangible. Intellectual property rights include the protections afforded to individuals and companies by governments through governments' granting of copyrights and patents, and through registration of trademarks and service marks. Online businesses must take care to avoid deceptive trade practices, making false advertising claims, engaging in defamation or product disparagement, and violations of intellectual property rights by using unauthorized content on their Web sites or in their domain names.

Domain Names, Cybersquatting, and Name Stealing

Considerable controversy has arisen recently about intellectual property rights and Internet domain names. Cybersquatting is the practice of registering a domain name that is the trademark of another person or company in the hopes that the owner will pay huge amounts of money to acquire the URL. In addition, successful cybersquatters can attract many site visitors and, consequently, charge high advertising rates. A related problem, called name changing, occurs when someone registers purposely misspelled variations of well-known domain names. These variants sometimes lure consumers who make typographical errors when entering a URL. Name stealing occurs when someone posing as a site's administrator changes the ownership of the site's assigned domain name to another site and owner.

Protecting Intellectual Property Online

Several industry trade groups have proposed solutions to the current problems in digital copyright protection, including host name blocking, packet filtering, and proxy servers. All three approaches illustrate how an Internet service provider might try to block access to an entire offending site. However, none of these approaches are really effective in preventing theft or providing identification of property obtained without the copyright holder's permission.

Defamation

A defamatory statement is a statement that is false and that injures the reputation of another person or company. If the statement injures the reputation of a product or service instead of a person, it is called product disparagement. In some countries, even a true and honest comparison of products may give rise to product disparagement. Because the difference between justifiable criticism and defamation can be hard to determine, commercial Web sites should avoid making negative, evaluative statements about other persons or products.

Advertising Regulation

In the United States, advertising is regulated primarily by the Federal Trade Commission.

The FTC publishes regulations and investigates claims of false advertising.

Information Included in FTC Policy Statements:

- Bait advertising
- Consumer lending and leasing
- Endorsements and testimonials
- Energy consumption statements for home appliances
- Guarantees and warranties
- Prices

Online Crime, Terrorism and Warfare

Crime on the Web includes online versions of crimes that have been undertaken for years in the physical world, including theft, stalking, distribution of pornography, and gambling. Other crimes, such as commandeering one computer to launch attacks on other computers, are new.

Law enforcement agencies have difficulty combating many types of online crime. The first obstacle they face is the issue of jurisdiction. Consider the case of a person living in Canada who uses the Internet to commit a crime against a person in Texas. It is unclear which elements of the crime could establish sufficient contact with Texas to allow police there to proceed against a citizen of a foreign country. It is possible that the actions that are considered criminal under Texas and U.S. law might not be considered so in Canada.

Another problem facing law enforcement officers is the difficulty of applying laws that were written before the Internet became prevalent to criminal actions carried out on the Internet.

Online Warfare and Terrorism

The Internet provides an effective communications network on which many people and businesses have become dependent. Although the Internet was designed from its inception to continue operating while under attack, a sustained effort by a well-financed terrorist group or rogue state could slow down the operation of major transaction-processing centers. As more business communications traffic moves to the Internet, the potential damage that could result from this type of attack increases.

Ethical Issues

Companies using Web sites to conduct electronic commerce should adhere to the same ethical standards that other businesses follow. If they do not, they will suffer the same consequences that all companies suffer: the damaged reputation and long-term loss of trust that can result in loss of business. In general, advertising on the Web should include only true statements and should not omit any information that could mislead potential purchasers or wrongly influence their impressions of a product or service. Even true statements have been held to be misleading when the ad omits important related facts. Any comparisons to other products should be supported by verifiable information.

Privacy Rights and Obligations

The issue of online privacy is continuing to evolve as the Internet and the Web grow in importance as tools of communication and commerce. Many legal and privacy issues remain unsettled and are hotly debated in various forums. The Electronic Communications Privacy Act of 1986 is the main law governing privacy on the Internet today. Of course, this law was enacted before the general public began its wide use of the Internet.

Ethics issues are significant in the area of online privacy because laws have not kept pace with the growth of the Internet and the Web. The nature and degree of personal information that Web sites can record when collecting information about visitors' page-viewing habits, product selections, and demographic information can threaten the privacy rights of those visitors.

Principles for Handling Customer Data:

- Use the data collected to provide improved customer service.
- Do not share customer data with others outside your company without the customer's permission.
- Tell customers what data you are collecting and what you are doing with it.

▶ Give customers the right to have you delete any of the data you have collected about them.

Communications with Children

In the United States, Congress enacted the Children's Online Protection Act (COPA) in 1998 to protect children from "material harmful to minors." This law was held to be unconstitutional because it unnecessarily restricted access to a substantial amount of material that is lawful, thus violating the First Amendment. Congress was more successful with the Children's Online Privacy Protection Act of 1998 (COPPA), which provides restrictions on data collection that must be followed by electronic commerce sites aimed at children. This law does not regulate content, as COPA attempted to do, so it has not been successfully challenged on First Amendment grounds. In 2001, Congress enacted the Children's Internet Protection Act (CIPA). The CIPA requires schools that receive federal funds to install filtering software on computers in their classrooms and libraries. Filtering software is used to block access to adult content Web sites. The Supreme Court held that the CIPA was constitutional in 2003.

Taxation and Electronic Commerce

An online business can become subject to several types of taxes, including income taxes, transaction taxes, and property taxes. Income taxes are levied by national, state, and local governments on the net income generated by business activities. Transaction taxes, which include sales taxes, use taxes, excise taxes, and customs duties, are levied on the products or services that the company sells or uses. Customs duties are taxes levied by the United States and other countries on certain commodities when they are imported into the country. Property taxes are levied by states and local governments on the personal property and real estate used in the business. In general, the taxes that cause the greatest concern for Web businesses are income taxes and sales taxes.

CHAPTER 10

Assurance Services

This chapter covers assurance services for electronic commerce consisting of the American Institute of CPAs' CPA Web Trust, and the Better Business Bureau (BBB) Online. The assurance services establish criteria and independent verification with regard to electronic commerce transactions. Standards established relate to the company and its business practices. An assessment is made of the controls in place to assure reliability and accuracy of transactions. A determination is made whether data is secure and protected from misuse. Consumers are very concerned about privacy and protection of personal information such as credit card numbers, social security numbers, and prior buying history.

CPA Web Trust Assurance Service

Trust Services (including WebTrust® and SysTrust®) are defined as a set of professional assurance and advisory services based on a common framework (that is, a core set of principles and criteria) to address the risks and opportunities of IT. Trust Services principles and criteria are issued by the Assurance Services Executive Committee of the AICPA.

The CPA (or CA) Web Trust provides approval and assurance of electronic commerce activities. An evaluation is made of commerce web sites to determine if they satisfy standards set by the American Institute of CPAs (in the United States) and the Canadian Institute of Chartered Accountants (in Canada). The American Institute of CPAs (AICPA) is the organization of certified public accountants (CPAs) while the Canadian Institute of Chartered Accountants is the organization of chartered accountants (CAs). CPAs and chartered accountants are licensed in their respective countries and are considered the same way for the purposes of this assurance service.

The number one priority with consumers is security when buying goods or services online. Customers are concerned with personal and financial information protection and confidentiality.

The CPA Web Trust informs prospective customers that a CPA has performed an appraisal of a Web site's policies and controls, and that the site is in conformity with appropriate conditions and practices. "Key" factors are examined for consistency, quality, and appropriateness. Privacy issues are addressed and appraised.

The major areas examined by The CPA Web Trust are:

▶ The protection and security of data. A determination must be made whether the Web site operator has workable controls and policies to assure that consumer information is protected from misuse. Information protection is enhanced when the business entity's servers use appropriate and up-to-date technology to encrypt private customer information. However, a problem with management control of sites is the failure of reports to reflect the workings of the server. CPA must assess for each site the encryption involved, digital IDs, and socket securing. Is the system secure? Content integrity is crucial particularly because of viruses and software counterfeiting.

▶ The integrity of transactions. An assessment is made whether the web site operator uses proper and effective controls over customer orders. Are the orders processed fully and correctly? Is the terms of sale and amount billed correct? Transaction integrity is fostered when transactions are accurate, validated, complete, identified, and timely. It is positive when the seller sends a customer a confirming e-mail message after the order is placed. Web Trust helps to minimize fraud on the Internet.

▶ Disclosures over business practices. A determination is made whether the Web site operator appropriately discloses its business policies over transactions. Are electronic commerce transactions with customers executed properly in accordance with its disclosed practices? What is the quality of customer service? How long does it take to fill an order? The site should list its shipping and problem resolution policies. In effect, the business practice disclosure mandates that the site specify how it will handle online transactions. The CPA does not provide any assertion about the products or services sold, the return policy, or warranties given.

The following should be done by the business entity in protecting online and other information dealing with electronic commerce:

▶ The business keeps a control environment conducive to meaningful control to protect customer data.

▶ There is a recurring monitoring by the business of procedures followed to assure they are working. If deviation from procedures or policies is noted, immediate corrective action is taken.

▶ The entity must keep control over transmissions of private customer information over the Internet from unexpected or unintended recipients.

- The business prevents unauthorized outsider access to restricted areas including the contents therein. If a customer accesses the Web page, the customer is restricted to customary activities such as making inquiries, executing transactions, and obtaining information about their transactions.
- The company does not disclose private customer information to parties unrelated to the entity's business unless customer permission has been received or customers have been notified before giving their information to the entity that such disclosure would be made.
- The entity has controls against improper access to the customer's computer and its content within. Customer data on their computers are not modified without their express permission. Further, customer approval is needed for any data storage or copying to their computer.
- The entity's employees do not use confidential customer information unrelated to their duties within the business.
- The entity has in place safeguards to assure that viruses are not transmitted to the customer's computer.

The following ways are involved in protecting against misuse of customer information in electronic commerce:
- Protect data once it reaches the business entity.
- Properly store, modify, and copy data on the customer's computer.
- Get the express permission of customers for the entity to use information for purposes other than for which it was given.
- Encrypt and safeguard private customer data such as credit card numbers.

The AICPA with the Canadian Institute of Chartered Accountants (CICA) introduced the CPA Web Trust seal. The seal is an assurance of quality and appropriateness for electronic commerce. Its purpose is to assure commerce Web sites satisfy minimum standards and criteria related to business practices, controls over transactions, and security of information. There is a monitoring and appraisal of Web business dealings to install customer confidence and trust. To obtain the seal, a business must undergo a thorough examination by a licensed CPA or chartered accountant. CPAs and CAs have a reputation for integrity, trust, and objectivity. The seal assures consumers that those Web sites having the CPA Web Trust Seal are reliable, accurate, and honest, and maintain confidential consumer information. To get and display the seal, the Web site must satisfy all CPA Web Trust Criteria. Web Trust engagements fall under AICPA statements on standards for attestation engagements. Web Trust is an international program.

There is an agreement between the AICPA and Veri Sign (a provider of digital authentication services including certificates). Veri Sign manufactured the CPA Web

Trust seal to be hard to forge and revocable in the event the entity does not satisfy the needed criteria. (Veri Sign is discussed in detail in a separate section).

Consumers desiring to make sure a site is certified can click on the seal and directly access a Veri Sign Web page to confirm the entity's status as duly approved. Further, by clicking on the seal the consumer may access the CPA's report and the CPA Web Trust principles and criteria.

Veri Sign digital identification shows web users that sites are representing themselves properly so customers can feel confident about the web site before they register on it, purchase from it, or browse.

Veri Sign certificates are such that encryption on it ensures that a third party can access the communications between the web site and customer. Digital certificates act as electronic credentials for the Internet and validate a business entity's identify for Web site security and reliability.

The addition of digital signatures to content distribution assures users of the quality of downloaded content.

Veri Sign will issue for a site a Secure Server ID for the Web Trust Program. There are about 35,000 Veri Sign Secure Server IDs for Web Commerce.

AICPA officials are widening their Web Trust standards to conform with privacy protection guidelines formulated by the Online Privacy Alliance (OPA), a coalition of American businesses established to promote safeguards and support self-regulation, and the European Union. The European Union (EU) has its own privacy protection rules which may limit electronic commerce activities between Europe and non-complying U.S. companies. OPA and EU guidelines require businesses to post notices on their Web sites of the type of personal information they are gathering electronically, and how such information will be used.

Only certain CPAs who have been licensed to perform Web Trust Examinations may do so. To find a list of CPAs who are licensed visit www.cpawebtrust.org.

Web Trust principles have to be satisfied. A CPA must satisfy the following requirements in order to provide this attestation service:
- Be a member of the AICPA.
- Have a license to do this service.
- Attend a special seminar.
- -Be subject to quality inspection.

To become Web Trust certified, the CPA should be competent in such areas as firewalls, communication protocols, hardware security devices, and server technology.

In performing this service, CPAs should have proper malpractice insurance coverage.

To get the seal, the business must be able to show that over at least two months and usually three months or more, that:

▶ Its controls were operational and effective.

▶ It keeps a control environment and has in place effective controls.

▶ There is a monitoring framework to assure that business practices are kept up-to-date.

▶ It did execute transactions in conformity with its disclosed business practices for electronic commerce transactions.

At a minimum, the CPA must examine each site quarterly and express continued approval. For dynamic Web sites, the CPA may have to visit the site more often than quarterly.

In conducting a Web Trust engagement, the CPA may facilitate his work by giving the company a self-assessment questionnaire. In completing the questionnaire, the company has to evaluate its online system including the control environment, and the way it processes and tracks orders. CPAs working with Web Trust can also get assistance from Internet service providers.

The Web Trust Seal of Assurance is an electronic seal attached to the Web site. The seal provides a level of assurance but is not a guarantee. If the CPA is assured that the web site has satisfied the criteria set forth by the CPA Web Trust, the CPA issues a report that compliance requirements have been met. The independent accountant's report clarifies what is or is not covered. To get the seal, the assurance provider (CPA) must issue an unqualified report on the Web site. The major aspect of the unqualified opinion takes the following form:

"Management's assertions regarding disclosure of business practices, transaction integrity, and information protection are fairly stated, in all material respects, in conformity with the authoritative Web Trust criteria set by the AICPA/CICA."

The business entity must post the online auditor's report. The report indicates the site's compliance.

Exhibit 10.1 below presents a full sample independent accountant's report.

Independent Accountant's Report

To The Management of ABC Company:

"We have examined the assertion by the management of ABC Company (ABC) on its Web site for electronic commerce (at www.ABC.com) during the period January 1, 2005 through March 31, 2005, ABC:

-- disclosed its business practices for EC transactions and executed transactions in accordance with its disclosed business practices,

-- maintained effective controls to ensure that customers' orders placed using EC were completed and billed as agreed, and

-- maintained effective controls to ensure that private customer information was protected from uses not related to ABC's business

in conformity with the AICPA/CICA Web Trust Criteria (hot link)." ABC's management is responsible for its assertion (hot link to management's assertion). Our responsibility is to express an opinion on management's assertion based on our examination.

Our examination was made in conformity with standards set by the AICPA. Those standards require that we plan and conduct our examination to obtain reasonable assurance that management's assertion is not materially misstated. Our examination included (1) obtaining an understanding of ABC Company's EC business practices and its controls over the processing of EC transactions and the protection of related private customer information, (2) selectively testing transactions executed in accordance with disclosed business practices, (3) testing and appraising the operating effectiveness of the controls, and (4) performing such other procedures as we considered necessary in the circumstances. We believe that our examination provides a reasonable basis for our opinion.

Because of inherent limitations in controls, errors or fraud may exist and not be detected. Further, projections of any evaluation of controls to future periods are subject to the risks that controls may become inadequate due to changes in conditions or that the effectiveness of such controls may deteriorate.

In our opinion, ABC management's assertion for the period January 1, 2005 through March 31, 2005 is fairly stated, in all material respects, in conformity with the AICPA/CICA Web Trust Criteria.

The CPA Web Trust seal of assurance on ABC's Web site for EC constitutes a symbolic representation of the contents of this report and it is not intended, nor should it be construed, to update this report or provide any additional assurance."

XYZ CPA Firm _____

Address _____

Date _____

It should be noted that the CPA's report should contain as a minimum the following:
- ▶ Whom the report is directed.
- ▶ State management's assertion.

▶ Enumerate the purpose of the engagement, the subject matter, and the time period covered.

▶ Discuss the responsibilities of management and the practitioner.

▶ Cite the relevant standards and criteria associated with the engagement.

▶ Provide a conclusion to the work performed including any reservations that may exist.

▶ Indicate the period covered and the date of the report.

▶ Provide the name and address of the CPA firm.

The public can access the criteria and principles set forth by the CPA Web Trust as well as the reports issued. Each CPA Web Trust site is linked to a directory of all sites having the seal of approval.

Information about Web Trust can be downloaded by accessing (http://infotech.aicpa.org/Resources/System+Security+and+Reliability/System+Reliability/Trust+Services) as well as www.cpawebtrust.org.

The Better Business Bureau (BBB)

Better Business Bureaus (www.bbb.org) are private, nonprofit entities supported mostly by membership fees paid by business entities and professional groups located in the geographic areas serviced by the Bureau. There are approximately 130 Better Business Bureaus located within the United States. Canada has about 20 Better Business Bureaus.

BBBs keep files on many businesses in their area and in fact some outside of their areas. BBB service areas can be found by entering a ZIP code online. Based on the ZIP code entered, the BBB servicing that area will be identified. The web page for the BBB will be displayed with relevant information such as whom to contact and overall policies.

The objectives of a BBB usually take the form of assuring quality products and services by members, promote customer education, engage in ethical activities, reliability and honesty, and voluntary self-regulation.

Membership in a BBB has the following benefits to the entity:

▶ BBB Decal, Plaque, and Certificate evidencing membership resulting in consumer confidence. The entity has greater credibility.

▶ Customer referrals through BBB service line or literature.

▶ Member "hotline" about companies, products/services provided, and professional advice. However, the BBB does not endorse any specific company, product, or service.

▶ The Alternative Dispute Resolution (ADR) staff aids in resolving complains and fostering customer "goodwill."

▶ Being Listed on the Internet including at reduced rates. Potential customers include those accessing the Internet directly or through online providers such as American Online, Prodigy, and CompuServe.

▶ Membership fees paid are tax deductible.

There are certain minimum requirements to qualify as a member of the Better Business Bureau as follows:

▶ Payment of fees.

▶ Provide background data about the entity and its principals.

▶ Furnish information about the entity's activities, reliability, and reporting.

▶ Be in business for at least 6 months unless either the principals previously operated an entity with a satisfactory record, the entity is a branch of a company that has met BBB standards, or the entity has agreed to a Pledge of Arbitrate agreement and/or an ADR precommitment program with the Bureau and is not involved in a business that has may complaints against it over time.

▶ Signing the membership application.

▶ Not have outstanding against it government actions related to consumer fraud or poor customer relations.

▶ Conform to BBB standards regarding advertising, promotion, and selling.

▶ Comply with arbitration findings by the BBB.

▶ Cooperate with the voluntary self-regulation within the entity's industry.

▶ Attempt to eliminate the courses of customer complaints.

▶ Meet the licensing and bonding requirements set by federal and local authorities.

▶ Respond quickly to complaints against the entity forwarded by the Bureau.

▶ Make reasonable effort to resolve customer complaints consistent with good business practice.

▶ Update information to the BBB annually.

▶ Do not improperly use the logo of the BBB such as for sales, advertising, or commercial purposes unless prior approval has been received.

Note: Some regional BBBs may place additional standards and requirements upon the entity.

The activities of the Better Business Bureau are:

▶ Emphasize ethical behavior in business.

▶ Self-regulate business practices.

▶ Furnish information concerning charities.

▶ Issue reports to business entities about consumers.

▶ Resolve disputes between the business and customers. In so doing, the resolution may be in the form of arbitration, mediation, or conciliation.

▶ Answer customer inquiries.

BBB reports are issued on all businesses which receive a lot of consumer inquiries or complaints. Reports are issued on both nonmembers and member BBB entities. If there is no BBB report on a particular company it means one or more of the following:

▶ Business activities have been minor.

▶ Complaints against the business are non-existent or minimal.

▶ It is a new business.

Information in BBB reports typically cover an activity period of 3 years and include:

▶ Nature and type of business.

▶ How long the company has been in business.

▶ How many years the BBB has evaluated the business.

▶ Whether the company has a pre-committed dispute resolution program.

▶ The complaint frequency, nature, and pattern, if at all.

▶ Whether federal or local government agencies have taken enforcement actions against the company. If so, why and what was the nature of the disposition. For example, has the company been fined by the U.S. Federal Trade Commission or state Attorney General?

▶ Whether the company is a member of the BBB.

There are two BBBs that make their reports available in separate databases online. They are:

▶ The BBB Covering Eastern Massachusetts, Maine, and Vermont.

▶ The BBB Serving Metropolitan New York, Mid Hudson, and Long Island Regions.

BBBs are located in practically every state (just click on the state when accessing through the Internet for specific information).

BBBOnLine (www.bbbonline.org)

BBBOnLine's mission is to promote trust and confidence on the Internet through the BBBOnLine Reliability and Privacy Seal Programs. BBBOnLine's web site seal programs allow companies with web sites to display the seals once they have been evaluated and confirmed to meet the program requirements.

Conclusion

In conclusion, the CPA Web Trust is concerned with evaluating security, privacy, and sound business practices. It provides independent third party verification of the web site by the CPA and the issuance of a report. There is a link from the Web site to such report. The CPA provides a Java applet (a kind of computer program used in the World

Wide Web). Participants in the Web Trust Program are entitled to display the seal on their sites. The Web Trust seal assures consumers that they are "safe" online. The certification seal is assurance to consumers of trustworthiness and integrity when doing business on the Internet. The seal is displayed on the Web site of the entity with a digital identification and expiration date. However, the seal is revocable if the entity at any time stops complying the Web Trust criteria. U.S. Federal Trade Commission guidelines may also apply. Web Trust has disclosure of a company's privacy policy, how privacy is enforced, and consumers are notified of what data is being accumulated about them.

Veri Sign helps to authenticate downloaded applications and content. The company concentrates on digital authentication products and services. Its digital certificates promote secure software distribution over the Internet.

A Better Business Bureau report is issued on businesses. The consumer should look at the report on a company before doing business with it. Does the business have a good or bad report? Why? How many complaints are there?

CHAPTER 11

Establishing a Presence on the Web and Business Online Strategies

Domain Names

A domain name is the part of the Internet address that is unique to you. It identifies your business and is used by others to access your web site. As an example, if the Internet address is "*http://www.yourcompany.com*," the portion that follows the "www." is the domain. The suffix ".com" stands for "commercial"; it denotes that the address belongs to a business or industry.

Other suffixes found in North American domain names are:
- .edu—for degree-granting colleges and universities.
- .gov—for agencies and branches of the U.S. government.
- .us—-used for state and local governments in the United States.
- .net—for entities that are part of the Internet's infrastructure. Intended for use by network information centers (NICs), network operations centers

(NOCs), administrative computers, and network node computers. The .net suffix is used worldwide.

- ▶ .org---for nonprofit organizations
- ▶ .tv—for television

Domain names for entities located outside North America generally do not end with .com, .edu, or .gov. The domain names for these organizations end with a two-letter suffix identifying the country of origin. For example, the Internet address *http://www.mycompany.ca* indicates that the site owner is based in Canada. Other international suffixes include:

Argentina	.ar	Israel	.il
Australia	.au	Italy	.it
Austria	.at	Japan	.jp
Bolivia	.bo	Liberia	.lr
Chad	.td	Netherlands	.nl
China	.cn	Nigeria	.ng
Finland	.fi	Pakistan	.pk
France	.fr	Russia	.ru
Greece	.gr	Spain	.es
Hong Kong	.hk	Switzerland	.ch
Iceland	.is	Trinidad/Tobago	.tt
India	.m	United Kingdom	.uk
Indonesia	.id	Vietnam	.vk
Ireland	.ie	Western Sahara	.eh

Registering the Name

InterNIC is the domain registrar, offering registration services and maintaining a central database of all Internet addresses and their registrants. InterNIC services are performed by Network Solutions Inc., in Herndon, Virginia *(www.internic.net)*. InterNIC works with domain administrators, network coordinators, ISPs and a variety of other users.

Network Solutions registers names and generates domain zone files for the Internet community. Network Solutions also helps users with policy and monitors the status of their registration requests.

Before registering a domain name, you need to see if that name has already been appropriated. This is where the WHOIS searchable database maintained by Network Solutions comes into play. Among other information, WHOIS lists domain names and the contacts associated with them for the .com, .edu, .net, and .org domains. You can use WHOIS not only to ascertain whether the name you want is available but also to find out who owns other names. Note that 'WHOIS' is not an acronym; rather, it is pronounced "who is."

Domains are registered online on the web site or via an FTP archive. New registration data is installed into the Domain Name System (DNS) root servers daily. Users not previously registered are given records in the WHOIS registry of applicants. (See Exhibit 11.1.)

Exhibit 11.1: The InterNIC Registration Process

1. Registrant fills out application.
2. Registrant e-mails application to hostmaster at InterNIC.
3. Request is acknowledged and assigned a tracking number.
4. Application is checked for errors.
5. InterNIC checks the WHOIS database to verify that the requested domain is available.
6. Application is processed and the registrant is notified via email.
7. Information for the new domain is added to InterNIC's WHOIS database.
8. InterNIC bills registrant for the domain registration.
9. Registrant pays invoice.
10. InterNIC sends registrant a renewal notice 60 days before the two-year anniversary of the initial registration.

However, for the typical business owner, domain registration directly with InterNIC is *not* possible because it requires a primary and a secondary server system. The requirement for this technology precludes most business owners from direct registration with InterNIC.

Using an ISP for Registration

You must therefore use an ISP to register a domain name. This is quite simple. The ISP site will have a search form that allows you to verify that the name you want is available, and you will typically be asked to provide:

1. Full name of contact.
2. Company name
3. Company description
4. Address
5. Telephone contact

179

6. Fax contact
7. Valid e-mail address
8. Web site password
9. Credit card information
10. Electronic signature of a licensing agreement.

The ISP will tell you what it will charge you for its domain registration service and should clearly inform you that you will get a bill directly from VeriSign for the first two years of domain registration.

Web Store Requirements

Most business-to-consumer e-commerce ventures take the form of retail business sites on the World Wide Web. The primary focus of such e-tailers is to develop, operate, and manage their websites to they become high-priority destinations for consumers who will repeatedly choose to go there to buy products and services.

Developing a Web Store

In order to launch your own retail store on the Internet, you must:

▷ *Build an e-commerce website.* Many companies use simple website design software tools and predesigned templates provided by their website hosting service to construct their Web retail store. Larger companies can use their own software developers or hire an outside website development contractor to build a custom-designed e-commerce site.

▷ *Develop your website as a retail Web business* by marketing it in a variety of ways that attract visitors to your site and transform them into loyal Web customers.

Serving Your Customers

Once your retail store is on the Web and receiving visitors, the website must help you welcome and serve them personally and efficiently so that they become loyal customers. Most e-tailers use several website tools to create user profiles, customer files, and personal Web pages and promotions that help them develop a one-to-one relationship with their customers. This can be done by:

▷ Creating incentives to encourage visitors to register
▷ Develop Web cookie files to automatically identify returning visitors
▷ Contracting with website tracking companies for software to automatically record and analyze the details of the website behavior and preferences of Web shoppers.

▶ Ensure that your website has the look and feel of an attractive, friendly, and efficient Web store.

Managing a Web Store

A Web store must be managed as both a business and a website, and most e-commerce hosting companies offer software and services to help you do just that. For example, service providers can offer their clients:

▶ A variety of management reports that record and analyze Web store traffic, inventory, and sales results.

▶ Build customer lists for e-mail and Web page promotions, or provide customer relationship management features to help retain Web customers. E-commerce software includes links to download inventory and sales data into accounting packages.

▶ Twenty-four hours a day and seven days a week operation all year long.

▶ Password and encryption protection of Web store transactions and customer records, and employ fire walls and security monitors to repel hacker attacks and other security threats.

▶ Provide clients twenty four hour tech support to help them with technical problems

Improving your Web site

Here are five things you can do to maximize your Internet presence.

▶ *Continually update your Web site.* This step is important to bring visitors back again and again, Also, search engines will check your site regularly and if the pages don't change, it can hurt your ranking in Web searches.

▶ *Add a Web log, or blog, to your Web site.* Not only does it help solve the problem of how to update your site, it can also draw more people to your site. Helpful content can help you gain return visitors. Plus, nothing can match a blog for keyword count, so it helps your search engine standing. Note: Some useful blog-related sites are: http://weblogs.about.com. www.blogger.com. www.trueblogging.com, www.technorati.com, www.blogwise.com, www. typepad.com, or www.eblogger.com

▶ *Keep it simple.* One of the biggest mistakes Web beginners make is creating a site that is too complicated. Forget the animations and dynamic content like stock tickers that increase the time it takes for your pages to open on a visitor's computer. In this same category, buy your own domain name so that your Web address will be easy to remember.

▶ *Be responsive to visitors.* If you offer a "contact us" page on your site, make sure someone responds promptly to the e-mails and phone calls that result.

Otherwise, your visitor will feel like the woman who walks into a brick-and-mortar store and can't find a sales clerk to help her.

▶ *Get help.* Seek professional help if you are not an expert at building or optimizing your Web site.

e-Commerce Success Factors

A basic fact of Internet retailing (E-tailing) is that all websites are created equal as far as the "location, location, location" imperative of success in retailing is concerned. No site is any closer to its customers and competitors offering similar goods and services are only a mouse click away. This makes it vital that businesses find ways to build customer satisfaction, loyalty, and relationships, to keep customers coming back to their Web stores.

The key to e-tailing success is to optimize factors such as:

▶ Selection and value
▶ Performance and service efficiency
▶ Look and feel of the site
▶ Advertising and incentives to purchase
▶ Personal attention
▶ Community relationships
▶ Security and reliability

Steps to Establish a Web Presence and do Business Online

▶ *Competitive landscape and strategic research*: look at your competitors online and decide how you will differentiate yourself from them.
▶ *URL*: register a domain name.
▶ *Technology*: buy a server or find an outsourced ISP.
▶ *Web development*: hire a web site developer or buy web development software, then determine site design and navigation.
▶ *Product or service*: create an online catalog or listings.
▶ *Payment*: find a secure online order solution, including shopping cart and payment service.
▶ *Security and protection*: fight viruses and protect the site and computers with anti-virus software.
▶ *Marketing*: develop a marketing plan which includes determining and publishing customer service policies (such as shipping and return policies).
▶ *Legal contracts*: establish alliances with crucial partners, such as product

suppliers, search engine optimizers, fulfillment services, shippers, web technicians, marketing or public relations firms.

▶ *Maintenance*: keep inventory, catalogs and listings up to date for your customers.

Source: Adapted from *Paypal's Guide to Doing Business Online, 2005* (www.entrepreneur. com/uploadedFiles/images/pdf/paypalbusinessonlineguide.pdf).

Glossary

ACQUIRING BANK bank that does business with sellers (both Internet and non-Internet) that want to accept payment cards.

ADDRESS RESOLUTION PROTOCOL aids network equipment and devices to ascertain an Internet protocol address.

ASYMMETRICAL DIGITAL SUBSCRIBER LINE protocol enabling substantial information delivery over copper telephone lines.

ASYMMETRIC CRYPTOGRAPHY means by which decryption and encryption occur using different keys.

AUTOMATED CLEARING HOUSE (ACH) electronic funds transfer system used in the United States to clear electronic payments for participating banks.

BACK-END PROCESSES computing usage for information kept on mainframe systems or services.

BLIND SIGNATURES Digi Cash System enabling one to receive e-cash from a financial institution but not correlating the name of the person with the token.

BLUETOOTH one of the first wireless protocols, designed for personal use over short distances.

BUSINESS MODEL a set of processes that combine to yield a profit.

BUSINESS-TO-BUSINESS (B2B) businesses sell products or services to other businesses.

BUSINESS-TO-CONSUMER (B2C) businesses sell products or services to individual consumers.

BUSINESS-TO-GOVERNMENT (B2G) businesses sell goods or services to governments and government agencies.

CABLE MODEM modem providing information transmission band widths not exceeding 30 Mbps using cable TV wiring.

CERTIFICATE AUTHORITY independent entity issuing and maintaining digital certificates for those on the Web who qualify.

CERTIFICATE REVOCATION LIST listing of participants on the Web who no longer qualify for digital certificates because of the problems which have arisen.

COMMON GATEWAY INTERFACE (CGI) SCRIPT scripting process for HTTP Web servers. The scrip typically allows for information to be exchanged between databases and a Web server. The coding language used for the scripts is Pearl.

CHARGEBACK the process that occurs when a cardholder successfully contests a charge and the merchant bank retrieves the money it placed in the merchant account.

CIPHER procedure to be followed in translating information in some code such as for security purposes. The encoded message is referred to as cipher text.

COMMON DATA SECURITY ARCHITECTURE (CDSA) cross-platform applications programming interface developed by Intel which acts at the system level. It enables cryptographic activities to be performed including algorithms of encryption. A uniform interface is used. Many companies are involved in this area of use such as Verisign, Netscape, and Datakey.

CRYPTO API programming interface that is application oriented developed by Microsoft. It allows for cryptographic functions. The modular nature of it provides for substitution in cryptographic algorithms. It can also be used in connection with digital certificates.

CRYPTOGRAPHIC ALGORITHM mathematical derivation integrating text with a series of digits (referred to as a "key") to generate unintelligible cipher text.

DATA ENCRYPTION STANDARD an algorithm or block cipher with a 56-bit key and functions in a 64 bit block. It is an expeditious way to encrypt voluminous data. IBM developed it.

DATA MINING looking for hidden patterns in data.

DIFFIE-HELLMAN an approach enabling two people to share a key to exchange messages. However, a drawback with this system is its failure of use with digital signatures or encryption.

DIGITAL CASH cash in electronic form.

DIGITAL CERTIFICATE document in electronic form issued by a trusted third party to substantiate the reliability of a vendor over the Internet or to state a business entity's identity by substantiating its public key.

DIGITAL SIGNATURE unique signing of electronic correspondence through encryption of a message along with the private key of the sender.

DISTRIBUTED COMPUTING ENVIRONMENT PROTOCOLS protocols related to the storage of software modules and its use on a network. It is typically used for authentication and for common interface applications on a network.

DOMAIN NAMING SERVICE service applicable to networks for the purpose of translating IP addresses in numeric form to text-based names.

DOUBLE-SPENDING spending a particular piece of electronic cash twice by submitting the same electronic currency to two different vendors.

ELECTRONIC CASH a general term that describes any value storage and exchange system created by a private (nongovernmental) entity that does not use paper documents or coins and that can serve as a substitute for government-issued physical currency.

ELECTRONIC DATA INTERCHANGE (EDI) standardized electronic exchange of documents among computers of different business entities. Business documents exchanged include sales invoices, purchase orders, quotes, credit memos for damaged or returned goods, and shipping reports. EDI transactions are usually between a buying company and its supplier.

ELECTRONIC FUND TRANSFER (EFT) mechanism facilitating the making of electronic payments between parties such as remittance advices among banks and direct deposits of salaries into the bank accounts of workers.

EXTRANET connection of two or more intranets among businesses. The extranet serves as a bridge between the public Internet and the private intranet. The extranet allows connection of multiple companies such as suppliers, distributors, contractors, customers, and trusted others behind virtual firewalls. These organizations can partner and share the network for transactions. Extranets provide a critical link between the extremes of the Internet and intranet. Extranets enable commerce through the Web at a very low cost and allow companies to maintain one-to-one relationships with their customers, members, staff, and others. The information on the extranet may be restricted to the collaborating organizations or may be available publicly. Extranets are flexible, scaleable, portable, and extensible. Extranets significantly reduce barriers to cross-organizational networking.

In summation, the extranet may be viewed either as part of a company's intranet that is accessible to other companies or as a collaborative Internet with other companies.

FIBER DISTRIBUTED DATA INTERFACE standard used in transmissions over fiber optic networks.

FILE TRANSFER PROTOCOL (FTP) protocol associated with the transfer of information on the Internet between client computers and file servers. Files may be transferred, downloaded, and uploaded individually or in batch form.

FINANCIAL EDI business-to-business EDI between businesses and their banks enabling banks to receive money from companies to pay suppliers, payees, utilities, etc.

FIREWALLS security controls for information transferred over a network between two parties. It provides protection against the misuse of data. It guards against protocols

187

or databases being compromised. However, firewalls do not safeguard a network against viruses nor assure authentication or privacy.

FRONT-END PROCESSES computer application using client computers attached to mainframes or servers.

GATEWAY software enabling two networks to connect and have data transfers between them even though there exist different protocols.

HYPERTEXT MARKUP LANGUAGE (HTML) uniform coding for defining Web documents. The browser used by the user examines the HTML to ascertain the manner in which to display the graphics, text, and other multimedia components. The use of HTML is recommended in developing intranets/extranets because it is easier to program than window environments such as Motif or Microsoft Windows. HTML is a good integrating tool for database applications and information systems. It facilitates the use of hyperlinks and search engines enabling the easy sharing of identical information among different responsibility segments of the company. Intranet data usually goes from back-end sources (e.g., mainframe host) to the Web server to users (e.g., customers) in HTML format.

HYPERTEXT TRANSFER PROTOCOL protocol which determines the way in which an HTML file is transmitted from server to client on the World Wide Web.

INTELLIGENT SOFTWARE AGENT (SOFTWARE ROBOT OR BOT) programs that search the Web and find items for sale that meet a buyer's specifications.

INTEGRATED SERVICES DIGITAL NETWORK (ISDN) global totally digital communications network using telephone lines. It has a lot of bandwidth.

INTERNATIONAL DATA ENCRYPTION ALGORITHM encryption algorithm with a 128-bit key.

INTERNET MAIL ACCESS PROTOCOL recent protocol for processing messages.

INTERNET PROTOCOL protocol for directing packets over an internetwork. It provides address space for internetworks.

INTERNET SERVICE PROVIDER (ISP) business to service customers so they may access the Internet such as Prodigy, CompuServe, and America Online.

INTRANET private network used within the company. An intranet serves the internal needs of the business entity. Intranet users are able to access the Internet, but firewalls keep outsiders from accessing confidential data. It makes use of the infrastructure and standards of the Internet and the Web. Intranets use low-cost Internet tools, are easy to install, and offer flexibility. Intranets have already been established by at least two-thirds of the Fortune 500 companies and many other organizations.

An intranet requires Web application development for its internal network such as appropriate Web servers. Quick response times require a direct connection to the server. The use of Web technology allows each desktop having a Web browser to access corporate information over the existing network. Employees in different divisions of the company located in different geographic areas can access and use centralized and/or scattered information. The major element in an intranet is the Web server software that runs on a central computer and serves as a clearinghouse for all information.

Intranet applications are scaleable - they can begin small and grow. This feature allows many businesses to "try out" an intranet pilot - to publish a limited amount of content on a single platform, and evaluate the results. If the pilot succeeds, additional content can be migrated to the intranet server.

Intranets provide access to external information resources including group access to mailing lists, threaded discussion groups, and stock/bond quotes.

IP ADDRESS identification of a computer in the network by a numeric address.

KEY sequence of digits which coupled with a cryptographic algorithm results in cipher text.

MARKET SPACE market in which electronic commerce is carried out.

MALWARE viruses, worms, Trojan horses, spyware, and adware.

MASHUPS the combining of output from two or more Web sites into a single user experience.

MICROCASH digital tokens of small denomination.

MICROMERCHANTS businesses on the Internet providing goods or services and receiving payment in digital cash or e-cash.

MICROPAYMENTS Internet payments for items costing from a few cents to approximately a dollar.

MICROTRANSACTIONS real-time transactions with microcash.

MIDDLEWARE software that processes transactions for a customer who is accessing many company databases.

MONEY LAUNDERING a technique used by criminals to convert money that they have obtained illegally into cash that they can spend without having it identified as the proceeds of an illegal activity.

MULTIMEDIA INTERNET MAIL EXTENSIONS protocol attached to e-mail messages comprising of two or more multimedia parts such as sound, video, and graphics.

NETWORK ACCESS POINTS on-ramp to the Internet such as that kept by Sprint.

ONE-WAY HASH FUNCTION process to translate a message into a message digest (string of digits). A key is not needed.

PACKET information grouping for transfer on a digital network. The packet is comprised of a bit sequence including both the actual data along with control data to assure proper transmissions.

PERSONAL DIGITAL ASSISTANT little portable device for electronic computing purposes.

POINTS-OF-PRESENCE in a domestic or global communications network, there are local access points. A local call will access the network. For example, a user of America Online dials a local telephone number but can access a global network of information.

POINT-TO-POINT PROTOCOL protocol for transmission involving serial modem usage.

POST OFFICE PROTOCOL protocol for e-mail on the Internet. It facilitates message retrieval.

PRETTY GOOD PRIVACY control of and security for e-mail transmission on the Internet. Encryption standards are used for a particular operating system. Prior to using e-mail software, encryption of the message may take place.

PRIVACY-ENHANCED MAIL safeguarding of e-mail via symmetric or public keys. However, this standard cannot be used with multimedia Internet mail extensions.

PRIVATE KEY key for encryption messages but the originator does not know what it is.

PROTOCOL guidelines and principles associated with the workings of a network. Rules surround data and electrical signals on the network, manner of information transmissions, accessing the network, and processing applications on the network.

PROXY SERVER used to safeguard key information and applications related to a network. Proxy servers cease the source's incoming connection and initiates a second connection to the destination. It assures that an incoming user has suitable access rights to use information asked for from the destination prior to having the information transferred to the user.

PUBLIC KEY key a receiver uses to decrypt a message. It is made public to interested parties as required.

PUBLIC KEY CRYPTOGRAPHY encryption approach utilizing both a private and public key. Encoded messages can be decoded with either key.

RADIO FREQUENCY IDENTIFICATION DEVICE (RFID) small chips that use radio transmissions to track inventory.

RC algorithm of RSA Data Security Inc. which utilizes ciphers for quick bulk encryption applications. This standard is faster than the Data Encryption Standard.

RSA public key encryption algorithm of RSA Data Security Inc. involving encryption of a variable key length and blocksize text. The text block is smaller than the key length. 512 bits is a customary key length.

SECURED ELECTRONIC TRANSACTION (SET) protocol used for both other applications (e.g., Web browser) and a standard to process over the Web credit card transactions.

SECURE HYPERTEXT TRANSFER PROTOCOL protocol supporting the hypertext transfer protocol. It fosters security, privacy, and authentication for data communications between a browser and a Web server.

SECURE MULTIMEDIA INTERNET MAIL EXTENSIONS (S/MIME) more recent standard of RSA Data Security Inc. utilizing cryptographic algorithms. It involves authentication from a certificate authority for digital certificates.

SECURE SOCKETS LAYER (SSL) protocol giving authentication, confidentiality, and information integrity when communicating. SSL security applies between the application layer and the transport and network layers. While SSL may also be applied to transactions outside of the Web it does not apply to authentication at the document or application level.

SECURE WIDE-AREA NETWORK protocol for authentication and encryption of packets including the management and exchange of keys. The protocol fosters interoperability between firewall vendors and router.

SIMPLE MAIL TRANSPORT PROTOCOL important Internet protocol in transmitting between servers e-mail messages.

SIMPLE NETWORK MANAGEMENT PROTOCOL protocol to control and manage network equipment including switching hubs, bridges, and routers.

SMART CARD small plastic card resembling a credit card with a unique embeddiment of an integrated circuit of electronic data. It provides security on who uses it, how it is used, and what data is contained or stored on it.

SOFTWARE AS A SERVICE business model whereby companies (such as Google, eBay, and Amazon.com) provide services based on their software, rather than providing software as a product (such as Microsoft Office).

SPOUFING individual pretending to be someone else on the World Wide Web or otherwise involving improper electronic transfer of information.

SYMMETRIC ENCRYPTION receiver and sender of electronic data use the identical key so either may encrypt or decrypt the information.

TAG in markup languages such as HTML and XML, notation used to define a data element for display or other purposes.

TCP/IP PROTOCOL protocol explaining the subdivision of information into packets for transmission, and the way in which applications involve transmitting e-mail and file transfer.

TELNET an Internet standard applying to remote host access and terminal emulation.

TOKENS string of digits for an amount of a particular currency. Each token is digitally stamped by the bank for authentication purposes.

TRADING PARTNER AGREEMENTS terms acceptable to two or more business entities in their business dealings that stipulate the type of data to be exchanged electronically among them.

TRANSACTIONAL COMMERCE customer transactions involving real-time interactivity with data contained in corporate data bases.

TRANSMISSION CONTROL PROTOCOL protocol determining the highest packet size and other attributes of the transmission. This protocol is designed if the objective is to have perfect transmission.

TRIPLE DES approach to encrypt a grouping of data three times with different keys each time.

UNIFORM RESOURCE LOCATOR (URL) approach to identify and describe a resource on the Internet. A URL starts with the protocol name to obtain the data from the server followed by the text name of the resource or IP address. As an example, a Web page is a resource requiring an HTTP protocol.

USER DATAGRAM PROTOCOL protocol defining the maximum packet (transmission) size as well as improving the transmission. If perfect transmission is not needed, it may be the way to go.

VALUE ADDED NETWORK private network applicable to electronic transfer of information among business partners.

VIRAL MARKETING a marketing method used in the Web 2.0 world in which users spread news about products and services to one another.

VIRTUAL CORPORATION company having employees in many different geographic localities who communicate with each other totally or mostly in electronic form.

VIRTUAL PRIVATE NETWORK private network that makes use of the Internet to save on costly leased telephone lines between offices.

WALLET aid to a Web browser involved in passing an encrypted credit card number between the buyer and seller. It is on the server of the credit card company (e.g., Cyber Cash) for approval after authentication has been made.

WEB 2.0 a loose cloud of capabilities, technologies, business models, and philosophies that characterizes the new and emerging business uses of the Internet. Software as a service is an example of Web 2.0.

WEB BROWSER software enabling one to hook up with network servers to obtain HTML documents and Web pages. It provides a linkage among pages and documents. The server may physically be on the Internet or a private network. The browser may contain "help" applications for special files.

WEB SERVER software that manages and controls information at the Web site. The program enables responses to be made to requests for information from Web browsers.

WIKI a knowledge base maintained by its users. It is processed on Web sites that allow users to add, remove, and edit content. The most famous wiki is Wikipedia, which is a multilingual, Web-based, free-content encyclopedia project.

XML (EXTENSIBLE MARKUP LANGUAGE) W3C's generic language for creating new markup languages. Markup languages (such as HTML) are used to represent documents with a nested, treelike structure. XML is a product of W3C and a trademark of MIT.

Index

How small businesses can stem huge losses from poorly-performing IT systems. With IT having now reached "utility" status everywhere, a firm's network infrastructure MUST be always in place to maintain its Internet access, computerization, phone system and a host of other mission-critical application. Companies can no longer function without these. Their customers, employees and vendors expect business networks to be fully functional, expeditious, security protected and accessible around the clock. This book addresses the implications of failing to insure that all your IT functions are "utility-status," and tells non-technical executives what needs to be done from a managerial perspective to achieve true utility status, as well as how to pro-actively monitor such functions to make sudden catastrophes a thing of the past. The book also provides case studies of companies who have lost money and business because they failed to heed this message.

ISBN: 978-1-906403-09-6   234 pages

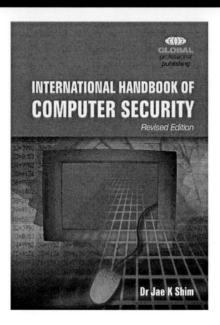

Computer security in the business environment can often seem a quagmire in which constantly changing hardware, networks, and software seem to create new problems all the time. *The International Handbook of Computer Security* is designed to help information systems/ computer professionals, as well as business executives, who have to protect their organization's computer systems and data from a myriad of internal and external threats while simultaneously ensuring it does not impact on productivity or work flow. Practical and thorough, the book addresses a wide range of computer security issues ranging from the hardware through software to the people involved.

ISBN: 978-0-85297-679-1   214 pages

Financial Services have always been based on one key resource:
information. Financial Service Organizations are about using
information to assess (or give probabilities) to future events.
Whether this is to predict mortality rates for life policy premiums,
which customers are likely to need a personal loan to buy their
next car, the rate to charge on a commercial loan, or to authorise
an individual credit card transaction, it all depends on the flow
of information. Ultimately, the quality of information and, a
businesses ability to extract value from it, is the key to competitive
success or even survival. Today, the free availability of and advance
of digital technology has only served to exaggerate the importance
of understanding and organising information.

ISBN: 978-1-84516-283-2   390 pages

HANDBOOK OF

Computer
Troubleshooting

• HARDWARE •THE INTERNET
• UTILITIES • GRAPHICS
• OPERATING SYSTEMS
• ERGONOMICS
• AND MUCH MORE . . . .

Michael Byrd
Jim Pearson
Robert A Saigh

More than just a quick-fix manual for the do-it-yourselfer, this book covers all aspects of small business computing. *The Handbook of Computer Troubleshooting* is a complete guide for solving the most typical problems most users will encounter. Both the new starter and the experienced user will find helpful tips to solve the more irksome, yet common, problems. Topics include: Hardware, Graphics software, the internet, Ergonomics, Keyboards, Networks, Company addresses, Utilities Software, Educational software, Printer, Monitors, Security Threats, websites, and much more. Michael Bird is an architect who has integrated computer networks into his design process. Jim Pearson is a systems integrator and engineer who consults with companies who implement e-business solutions. Robert A Saigh is a full-time writer with an extensive background in software training and technical writing.

ISBN: 978-1-888998-99-3   288 pages

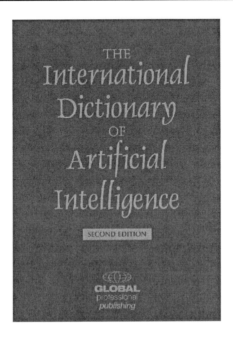

THE
International
Dictionary
OF
Artificial
Intelligence

SECOND EDITION

GLOBAL
professional
publishing

Anticipating the needs of professionals and researchers alike, this Dictionary is the first up-to-date reference volume on a discipline of ever-growing importance. Artificial intelligence is rapidly becoming the foundation discipline for thousands of new applications and will have dramatic effects on virtually every activity in which we engage. This essential reference features over 2,500 entries, all defined and explained and illustrated, as well as detailed explanations of major concepts in related disciplines. A completely cross-referenced index, annotated bibliography, and extensive appendix of World Wide Web sites on the latest trends in AI, all will make this a favourite resource for practitioners and researchers around the world.

ISBN: 978-0-85297-657-9   240 pages

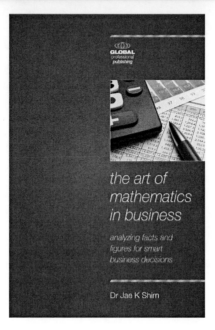

This book is a comprehensive, one-stop desk reference for managers and owners of small businesses who must use quantitative calculations to make daily operating and investing decisions. Its purpose is to provide the fundamentals of business maths techniques that can be quickly applied to real-world problems. This unique resource will save countless hours of research time by making sound financial planning truly easy. It provides analyses as well as clear and understandable explanations of complex small business problems. Basic mathematical techniques are presented in a step-by-step fashion that takes the reader through each stage of the problem-solving process. The examples in this book provide an invaluable and effective operating tool. This book also contains user-friendly personal computer techniques. The examples enable the businessperson to measure results and to report the data in an easy-to-understand format.

ISBN: 978-1-906403-32-4   406 pages

GLOBAL
professional
publishing

The Businessman's
CASH FLOW
HANDBOOK

Cash, Credit and Collections

Jeannette Cloud CBF

'Profits are an opinion, but cash is a fact'.

Never were truer words ever spoken. Is it possible for profitable companies to go out of business? Absolutely. A successful business is not successful without ensuring that their cash flow is positive: you cannot pay the rent, order supplies and inventory or pay employees without the regular receipt of cash. In fact executives can find themselves facing legal action and penalties if they trade when unable to pay the companies debts. This book will help you learn how to keep your company on solid ground by emphasizing the basics and ensuring that everyone in the organization understands the importance of cash flow.

ISBN: 978-1-906403-01-0   164 pages

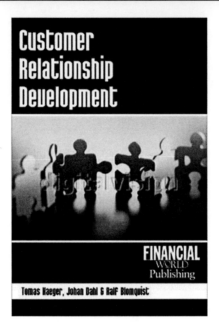

A practical guide to achieving value from customer knowledge
and applying it to develop better relationships with customers,
better targeting of marketing effort and increased cross-selling.
The book's importance lies in real experience of achieving
success using customer knowledge. With the perceived failure
of many large-scale CRM initiatives, the principles of CRM
have been difficult to achieve in the real world. CRD is aimed
at providing a guide for the rapid implementation of customer
management techniques to quickly achieve an increase in
cross-sale ratios and improved customer satisfaction. Using the
processes described this can be achieved for a relatively small
initial investment.

ISBN: 978-0-85297-682-1   176 pages

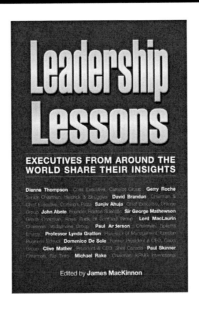

This book has captured the experiences of world-class business leaders, and pass this know-how to the next generation. The hard-won lessons they have learnt throughout their careers form the foundation of this book and these lessons will give guidance and help across the spectrum of management. The lessons cover major issues in Strategy, Change, Motivation, Teams, Developing People and Leadership. Contributors include:-

Gerry Roche, Senior Chairman, Heidrick & Struggle
Dianne Thompson, Chief Executive, Camelot Group
Sir George Mathewson, Group Chairman, Royal Bank of Scotland
Sanjiv Ahuja, Chief Executive of Orange Group
Clive Mather, President & Chief Executive, Shell Canada
Michael Rake, Chairman, KPMG International
Paul Skinner, Chairman of Rio Tinto
Domenico de Sole, Former President & CEO of Gucci Group
Professor Lynda Gratton, Professor of Management, London Business School.

ISBN: 978-0-85297-770-5   132 pages

Can compliance be turned into a competitive advantage, rather than a driver of costs? Are financial institutions merely passive recipients of government intervention or is it possible for smart corporates to play a role in shaping regulation and compliance, nationally and internationally?

This book addresses these challenges and explores all these opportunities. It provides a detailed guidance for those who are responsible for designing and applying compliance regimes in companies. Understanding the context is essential to anyone wishing to extract value from compliance, possibly turning a cost centre into a competitive advantage.

Topics covered include legislation, self-regulation, contractual arrangements, embedded regulation, hybrid models, enforcement, emerging trends and the role of regulation in society and finance.

ISBN: 978-1-906403-02-7   224 pages

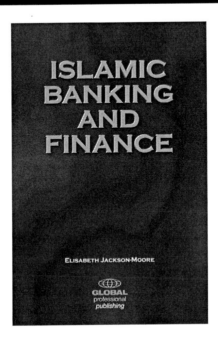
The International Handbook of Islamic Banking and Finance will give conventional bankers and financial advisers a detailed insight into Islamic banking. The book explains how it operates, what is the rationale behind it, the issues it raises, issues of compliance and how Islamic methods of banking relate to conventional banking and finance as well as the opportunities it presents.

While covering the ethical and religious basis of Islamic banking, Elizabeth Jackson-Moore concentrates on the details of how it provides all the services of any banking system. Financing instruments, Islamic contracts, Islamic bonds, *Takaful* (basically Islamic insurance) as well as new developements in Islamic banking such as hedge funds.

All compliance and regulatory issues are covered from an international point of view and the author also surveys the world banking centres.

ISBN: 978-1-906403-31-7   272 pages